Controversial and acclaimed in its British, New Zealand, and German editions, this dazzling hybrid of travel writing and imaginative writing is now being published for the first time in the U.S.

In 1991, with communism in tatters throughout Eastern Europe, Lloyd Jones took it into his head to journey halfway around the globe to a most unlikely destination: Albania. (He was intrigued in particular by stories of a village dentist who had served as a look-alike double of the late Albanian dictator at countless public appearances for twenty years.) What Jones found at every turn in Albania was a relentlessly bizarre world of half-truths and fictions. In that world, your status and sometimes your life hinged on your *biografi*: the security dossier that was maintained on you and consulted —or reinvented—to suit the moment.

From this world of distorted mirrors now being shattered by the twists of history, with every individual and the country as a whole being forced to reimagine an identity, Jones has constructed a compelling traveller's tale indeed: a travelogue both real and imaginary (could it be otherwise?) that unforgettably guides the reader into a mesmerizing, shocking—and often grimly funny—culture of illusion and deceit, the culture of biografi.

Lloyd Jones, a New Zealander, is the author of two novels and the short-story collection *Swimming to Australia*, which was short-listed for New Zealand's top literary prizes. He lives in Wellington.

ALSO BY LLOYD JONES

Swimming to Australia

BIOGRAFI

A Traveller's Tale

LLOYD JONES

A Harvest Original
Harcourt Brace & Company
SAN DIEGO   NEW YORK   LONDON

Requests for permission to make copies of any part of the work should
be mailed to: Permissions Department, Harcourt Brace & Company,
6277 Sea Harbor Drive, Orlando, Florida 32887-6777.

First published in Great Britain in 1993 by Andre Deutsch Limited.

Library of Congress Cataloging-in-Publication Data
Jones, Lloyd, 1955–
    Biografi: a traveller's tale/Lloyd Jones.— 1st U.S. ed.
    p.   cm.
    "A Harvest original."
    ISBN 0-15-600128-4
    1. Shapallo, Petar.   2. Imposters and imposture—Albania.
  3. Hoxha, Enver, 1908–1985.   4. Albania—History—1944–1990.
  I. Title.
  DR977.25.S52J66   1994
  949.6503'092—dc20   94-25467

This text was set in Joanna.

Designed by Kaelin Chappell
Printed in the United States of America
First U.S. edition 1994
A B C D E

The author gratefully acknowledges the assistance of a travel bursary and "scholarship in letters" from the Queen Elizabeth II Arts Council of New Zealand.

BIOGRAFI

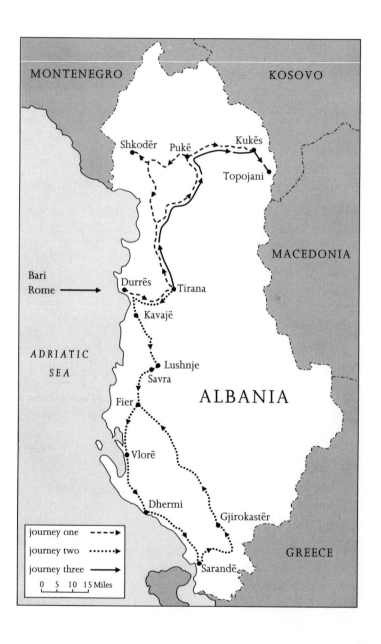

1

I was looking for Petar Shapallo but the face that had been Petar Shapallo's had vanished under a surgeon's knife. So I was left with the name which few people remembered, and a face fewer still had seen.

The shoemaker in Rruga November 17, for instance, said, "Yes, I know this man. We were at school together."

And after that?

The man shrugged. "You asked if I knew him."

He thought some more.

"Petar," he said, "was very good at gymnastics."

Kindly and well-disposed towards his mother, the shoemaker added.

"He was a dentist," I said.

"I did not say that," said the man.

"I know. I'm saying it. The Petar Shapallo we are looking for was a dentist."

"If he was a dentist, then go to the dentists' union. As you can see, I am a shoemaker."

The dentist had had the misfortune to be born in the very same month as the Balkan dictator Enver Hoxha.

A shared birthday wasn't necessary—but one can see how it might have helped in making the dentist a persuasive candidate. The moon entering the third phase, the alignment of the planets . . . that sort of thing. More important was the fact of Shapallo's size. He was over six feet tall, and broad across the shoulder. The dentist and the dictator had perfect matching shadows. And twin smiles designed to reassure. I had heard it said: People who saw a smile cross Enver's face were often surprised to learn that he was ordering their execution. But just as misleading was Shapallo's smile—that grin of a man caught in the rain without a coat or umbrella the moment he learned he was required to perform a special duty at the highest level.

Height, breadth, and smiling lines—these are the vital ingredients. The rest the surgeon sculpted. Hairdressers and tailors worked on Shapallo to improve the resemblance. The dictator occasionally looked in on the work-in-progress. His glance moved between Shapallo and his own reflection in a hand-held mirror. Once satisfied that the reflection could not be improved, he had Shapallo's family killed—his wife and two daughters, ages eight and ten. Next to go were the surgeons, hairdressers, and tailors. They were in the bus that toppled over the cliffs which spill down to Dhermi on the Adriatic Coast.

The years passed. Shapallo, as it happened, was spared the assassin's bullet and the dictator died in the mid-eighties, disabled by Parkinson's, a frail shadow of the comparatively robust Shapallo filling in for him on the podium. There was a ceremony for retired border guards at which Shapallo pinned medals to the chests of the veterans at the very same moment that the dictator lay on his deathbed. The death notice arrived several days later. The announcer's voice on

Radio Tirana was solemn and grave. The grieving process thus began.

To commemorate the loss of the Great Leader an extra "attack day" was declared in the countryside. In Tirana people lined up to give parting kisses. They wept and threw themselves over the coffin. A woman screamed for her heart to be torn open and for Enver to be fed with her blood. This "correct" display of emotion was shown many times on Albanian television. Each time, a soldier with a rifle slung over his shoulder prises the woman from the coffin. The woman is led to a chair, and the line of mourners takes a step forward. On it went—until the day of entombment arrived with the rumoured sighting of the Great Leader; like the "Christ figure," Enver had risen from the dead.

The sightings spread out from Tirana to the countryside, along the coast: Vlorë, Himore, Borsh, Sarandë. Eyewitness reports spoke of a man with "film-star looks." It was quiet for a spell; then a woman in Korcë recalled that, before she fainted, a man exactly like the Great Leader had tapped her on the shoulder and asked for water. This man, she said, had been exceptionally polite.

There were several more mountain sightings—the last one in a small village tucked at the bottom of the Coraun range, which is the peaked hat on the Karaburun peninsula separating the muddy Adriatic from the Ionian Sea.

The last sighting, and the one that lent credence to all the others, had come from a German embassy official in the aftermath of the rush on the foreign embassies in Tirana. In June 1990 the regime casually announced that passports could as of now be obtained from the Ministry, the extraordinary implication being that everyone was now free to travel. The controls along Embassy Row were relaxed. At first no one wished to appear too eager. Second or third in line was okay, but to head a line was risky. Along Embassy Row people began to gather. For the time being everything was orderly. But then the rumour spread beyond Tirana that the embassies were taking people in, and the dribs and drabs grew to a torrent of new arrivals. All through the night and the following day the crowd built. People arrived by train, by bus, by cart; they walked in from outlying villages. They were a crowd now and as such a powerful new voice emerged. Graffiti appeared on the stone walls comparing Hoxha with Hitler. Outside the embassies the crowd chanted the new words: "Freedom. Democracy." The police fired shots in the air. They tried to shout the crowds down with the use of megaphones.

It was during the second night that Shapallo managed to climb over the iron fence into the grounds of the German embassy. A good number of fellow travellers were already huddled under blankets and Shapallo was able to wriggle down in a bed of gravel.

He came to at first light with a boot in his ribs. Then something hard—a fist or paling—struck his forehead. A woman screamed in his face: "Murderer!" He was barely awake to the fact that he was being kicked, shoved, and punched back to the iron railing. Word passed among the crowds camped along Embassy Row that the ghost of the late dictator had come back to haunt and burden with guilt those seeking to leave. There was a terrible commotion. Soldiers fired shots in the air to try to break up the crowd. Shapallo was pinned to the fence inside, and those on the outside waiting to get into the embassy reached through the fence to rip his clothing. It was left to embassy officials to haul the concussed dentist to safety inside the building. A doctor was sent for—and an earlobe was sewn back on and several cuts stitched above Shapallo's right eye. Two ribs had been broken and a plug of hair ripped out from his left temple.

2

The story Shapallo told Gert Munz, the consulate chargé d'affaires, resulted in a few paragraphs published in the West. It told of a dentist with memories as Petar Shapallo being obliged to travel behind darkened windows, to present himself on balconies to the cheering masses on May Day; and once, when the leader dreamt of an airplane crash, the dentist had been obliged to take the leader's place on a helicopter flight from Vlorë to the then Russian naval base nearby.

Shapallo had been given new shoes, new clothes, books. He was told to favour his left leg when walking. In the event of an unscheduled encounter with the public he was told to reminisce about his childhood. He should begin by staring off into the distance and recite, "When I was a boy . . ."

Shapallo was the perfect shadow. He lost weight when the Great Leader dieted; together their hairlines receded, and when the Great Leader sprained an ankle, Shapallo limped. On film, Shapallo is the slow-moving shadow turning to wave to the crowd; there, he pauses from his stride to take a bouquet of flowers from a small girl. Here, he strikes a serious pose. He tilts back his chin and clasps his hands behind his back: but, on film, is he thinking as an emperor or as a dentist?

That first night in the embassy the concussed dentist awakes in darkness. He sits up in bed and wonders where he is—what are these mattresses made of? His hands touch his chin, his eyes, his cheeks—but inevitably locate the profile of the late and disgraced leader.

A staff member found him the next day, draped over the bathtub, the mirror and bathroom walls splattered with blood and, in the handbasin, the knife which Shapallo had taken to the Emperor's face.

Shapallo has lost the tip of his nose. Down the centre of his forehead he has made a deep cut. It was Munz's impression that the dentist had tried to peel back the skin. Twice Shapallo had plunged the knife deep into the cheekbone beneath his left eye, but he'd lost consciousness before the tip of the knife was able to locate the eye socket.

In Tirana the Party leaders are dismayed. They shake their heads, like disappointed parents. They speak out against the senseless vandalizing of life and property. In soft voices they say, "Look at this. And that. Over there . . . Why?"

The buses have been set on fire. The windows in the buses and trains are smashed. The huge greenhouses in the countryside lie in tatters. Shattered glass gathers in the schoolyards.

At the city zoo the tracks of a children's train wind in and out of the charred remains of animals spit-roasted over open fires. Behind locked bars the lions have shrivelled up under mounds of skin and fur, hunger's sleep. Vagrants have succeeded, though, in forcing their way inside the monkey cages, and chimp bones lie in small blackened piles in the chestnut groves of the zoo park.

The bird cages are also empty. And the two big soft eyes gazing up from a pile of chestnut leaves belong to the bony head of a seal. The animal has been dragged a couple of hundred metres from its rockery and filleted. The last surviving animal in the zoo is a languorous rhino. I watch the zookeeper feed it hay on the end of a pitchfork. He looks up, aware suddenly that he has company. The zookeeper sees me and draws a finger across his throat.

3

On my second day in Tirana a young medical student shows me where the statue of Stalin had stood. The key, he says, to blowing up a statue is knowledge of anatomy. Earnestly he explains how two tonnes of gelignite placed by the tyrant's feet will blow off the toes, but this, of course, amounts to no more than a glancing blow. In the fold of the dictator's arm a stick of gelignite will blow an arm sky-high—a crowd-pleaser for sure. But for the ultimate result a stick of gelignite must be placed in a hole drilled over the heart.

"Over the heart. You understand?" And he jabs a finger in my chest—so that I may better understand.

The medical student had been amazed to discover that

the Emperor's statue in downtown Tirana had been hollow and badly welded.

But none of these student interpreters has shown much heart for tracking down Shapallo. They stick to the Tirana they know. And, understandably, their preoccupation is with other things.

It is November and unseasonably cold. Each morning the city awakes to ice on the pavements and the small fires of the gypsy streetcleaners. People talk of the approaching winter. It is like a medieval fear of what lies to the lee of the mountain. Old men sit around in cafés which have no food to offer. They smoke their last cigarettes, and long after the silty coffee has hardened to a rind in their cups they joke amongst themselves as to who will still be around by the end of winter.

This Shapallo, they ask, has he been working in Greece? Has he brought back supplies? Has he some good raki from Kosovo to sell? Does he know where we can find some cheap fuel? Why, they ask, should they know this man-lizard? This chameleon? Or else they ask again, who is it exactly that I am looking for, a dentist or an emperor?

We have had enough of emperors, they say. It's dentists we need, and the undeniable truth of this is there to be seen in the few cracked teeth straggling to the bitten corners of their mouths.

At such moments I can feel the willingness of my student interpreters crumble beside me.

One such experience. After the guffawing subsides, an old man follows me out of the café behind the Tirana Hotel and takes hold of my coat sleeve. He begins to tell me something, and I redirect him to the interpreter, who is very excited: "This man here, he has heard of this person Shapallo." This is too good to be true. But there's the man's whiskery grin. There he is, nodding, full of assurances. "Shapallo," he says. Then off he goes—explaining something at great speed. "Yes," says the interpreter slowly. "There is such a person who can assist with information. A shoemaker."

Some years earlier I first came upon "Bird the First, King of the Sons of the Eagle," buried away in the Talk of the Town section of *The New Yorker*. Ahmed Bey Zogu was born in 1895. In 1925 he became President of Albania, and three years later he was proclaimed King Zog. For his coronation he ordered an outfit which included rose-coloured breeches, gold spurs, and a gold crown weighing in at nearly eight pounds.

But not even the most expensive finery succeeded in convincing all of his legitimacy, and for the duration of his reign King Zog's preoccupation was "staying alive." In all, he survived fifty-five assassination attempts. The first one came in 1931: a burst of gunfire greeted Zog as he left a Vienna opera house after a performance of *Pagliacci*. Although one particular assassination attempt did much to turn him into a national hero, when, as President, he was wounded three times outside the Parliament in Tirana. Without thought to his injuries Zog calmly walked back inside to the Parliamentary Chamber and, ignoring his bleeding, gave one of the "most brilliant speeches of his career [and] the longest."

A king, of course, requires a queen. It is one of life's symmetries. Like salt and pepper. So Zog commissioned his four sisters, each princess a division commander in the Albanian Army (and none married themselves), to find him a suitable spouse.

A single photograph of a penniless half-American, half-Hungarian countess, Geraldine Apponyi, who had been selling postcards in the Budapest National Museum for forty-five dollars a month, captured the King's heart.

One year after the marriage, Italy invaded Albania. The Royal Household fled to England as first Mussolini's Fascists, followed by the Germans, and in 1944 Enver Hoxha's Communists took over the kingdom, formally deposing the King *in absentia* in 1946.

King Zog wasted no time in setting about the royal circuit. He was a friend of King Farouk. In Alexandria the Albanian King and Queen danced in the gardens of Farouk's summer palace. There were bridge and tennis parties to attend with other royal exiles.

In 1951 the King toured the United States and bought Knollwood, a grand Long Island residence. Italian Renaissance in style, it boasted several kingly attributes—tall Ionic columns and a winding stairway of marble. For the duration of Zog's residence a bearded Royal Guard was stationed at the gate—he would kiss the hands of visitors and gently turn sightseers away.

In 1952 the King was unable to convince the Nassau County authorities that as a monarch he had "sovereign immunity" from such trifles as paying taxes.

Three years later he sold Knollwood. Its grounds were ripped up by vandals in search of the gold Zog was rumoured to have escaped Albania with and buried in the gardens of Knollwood. The mansion was later demolished. In the late sixties Nassau County acquired Knollwood and incorporated it into a wilderness reserve.

King Zog spent his last years drifting in and out of pain caused by his illness and dreaming of his restoration to the throne. He died in 1961 in Foches Hospital, Paris, broken in body and spirit. But not forgotten.

In 1990, a man living with an Australian wife in a ranch-style home outside Johannesburg issued a press release saying that he was Leka I, son of "Bird the First, King of the Sons of the Eagle," and that he was ready and willing to assume the throne of Albania.

4

In a number of ways the Balkans had obtruded into my world. My summers had been spent in a place called Kansas Street in the Wairarapa, New Zealand, where my uncle had as a neighbour Cliff Dalziel. "A talented man," it was often said of Cliff, but ruefully, as though the promise of Cliff's talent had coved off to disappointment.

Cliff was a shortwave-radio operator. All his waking hours were spent in a shed playing with his radio gear. There was no boundary fence or hedgerow to speak of, and summer evenings I lay in the dry straw-like grass eavesdropping on Cliff while he worked his dials through the clouds of static, waiting for him to hit a pocket of sound, so pure and nearby that it often felt as though the voice of Radio Tirana had arrived at the bottom of the Pacific from the other side of a wall in a cheap motel room. Sometimes we heard Albanian or Greek music wavering out of Cliff's shed. The song grew dim and faded and the static returned. Cliff would chase after it and try to woo it back with the dials but the song was gone. Then, maybe, the announcer's voice would come through strong—it was 92 degrees in Tirana. An astounding heat which I associated with older civilisations. In our part of the world heat got tossed around by winds twisting out of valleys and rushing across farmland.

I lay back on the lawn trying to imagine a heat that came out of a kiln. Then the voice from Tirana vanished inside a thin whistle out to the stratosphere, and from inside the tin shed I heard Cliff read out the time on his wristwatch: "Eight-thirty, February nine, nineteen hundred and sixty-three." The transmission was recorded in a school exercise book which he carried to and from the shed.

There was a national league for shortwave-radio buffs. Cliff had cartons full of QSL cards—these were verification cards—from the Venezuela telephone system, from a German institute of physics; he once showed me a slightly terse letter from the Israelis reminding Cliff that "their transmission was not intended for reception by the general public." A 1970 letter from Radio Peking provided Cliff with a proud moment. The letter read: "Thank you for your letter and your congratulations to our country on the successful launching of the first man-made earth satellite . . . Our great leader Chairman Mao [has] pointed out, 'The era in which Chinese were regarded as uncivilised is now over.' "

Cliff said he wasn't competitive about it, although

within the league and amongst some members there was quite a bit of argument as to what was or wasn't a country. To earn points you had to tape a transmission. The champion shortwave-radio operator with virtually an unassailable lead was a blind man who lived with his elderly sister at the bottom of the South Island.

For Cliff it had started out during the war, when he was a ship's radio officer sailing in the Adriatic. Each night he listened in to "fellco radio," used by the partisan groups inside Albania and Yugoslavia. After the war he wrote to those countries on whom he had eavesdropped—and with what I imagined to be a pen pal curiosity, Albania had written back.

For twenty-eight years Cliff monitored Radio Tirana's broadcasts. The clearest signal was the daily broadcast, which was aimed at America but which sometimes overshot, to land in the Pacific.

But Cliff had also taken it upon himself to expand his duties to other things.

For nineteen years he paid rent on a small shop display in the world trade centre. The Soviets also had a prominent but largely ignored window front. Mothers with prams lost in the maze of the centre's corridors and wings suddenly found themselves confronted by Cliff's Albanian window: dolls in folk costume, a bottle of raki, a plastic bunch of grapes. And for a colourful backdrop Cliff had mounted on display boards photographs of women in white cotton head-dresses working in the fields. Lean, healthy-looking farm-workers waved from the seats of tractors. Happy miners waved back along dark and narrow mine shafts.

Cliff and his wife, Bess, had a daughter and a son. We had not been close. I knew only the daughter's name, Grace. A crucial five or six years separated us. Her older brother left home and Grace was gone less than eighteen months later. My memories are of Grace studying till all hours, and of the bright halo her desk lamp created in the window. Once Grace left, it felt as though the Dalziel children had simply passed on to another world. I never saw them or heard them mentioned by their parents.

Driving to Cliff's place, after all these years, I couldn't think of the son's name. But as I pulled outside the Dalziel house, in another part of my memory I saw him quite clearly—eighteen or nineteen years of age he must have been, standing outside his house and staring in the windows unsure as to whether he had locked eyes with a friend or a stranger.

I parked and spent a moment looking at my uncle's old house. Smaller, plainer than I had remembered. The new owners had let the garden go. On Cliff's side of the boundary the tin shed was gone, although a very tall radio aerial rose at the side of the chimney.

I was intending to go to Tirana and I had a manila folder of photographs to show Cliff—of young men, naked to the waist, dragging themselves from the water in the Albanian port of Durrës. There was a boat going to Italy and everybody wanted to be on it. In the photographs people cling to the sides of freighters. Others are climbing up ship ropes. There is one photograph of a woman with a baby tied to her belly; she is hauling herself and the child, hand over hand, up the rusted side of a freighter. The harbour is white with splashes. According to the photographs, bodies fall like torpedoes—resignedly and without fuss. Among the crowd gathered on deck there is no excitement. There doesn't appear to be any backslapping—or even the "Thank God, we've made it" sentiment which you might expect. Instead, the crowd in this photograph reminded me of high jumpers, successful so far, but for the moment content to sit on their haunches to see who else will make it.

The other Reuters photographs were of exhausted men and women resting on a mountain pass high up in the winter snow and ice of the Pindus Mountains. Men, women, children, small babies swaddled in blankets, walking the "freedom corridor to Greece."

Cliff was dismissive. The photos were of "good-time boys wanting jeans and discotheques." The country was in the hands of reactionaries. Everything had gone to hell.

He spoke of the country falling to saboteurs, foreign agents, Fascists. Extravagant language which pressed the buttons to another era—to grainy films of the forties, of smoky rooms, women with obscure accents, troubled intellectuals who dabbled in explosives. And yet Cliff was none of these things. The last time I had had a studied look at him was two years previously. A photo had appeared in the local newspaper of Cliff staring gravely back at the community. In the foreground was a cake with lit candles to mark the woodwork teacher's retirement. It was a straightforward head and shoulders, but you knew there was a flat carpenter's pencil stuffed down the inside of his walk socks. I also seemed to recall a scar on his knee from a brush with a lathe. Most of all, you sensed that the frosty distance between the blackboard and the first row of desks would accompany

Cliff into private life. It had to do with his bushy eyebrows, I think. His eyes, sheltered underneath that stiff ridge, gazed out over the classroom, suspicious, and forever sensing laughter behind his back.

Bess, Cliff's wife, pushed open a door in the side of the house and called out, "Cliff . . . You have a visitor."

She leant around the door as if reluctant to enter. "Shall we say fifteen minutes?" Then to me: "I bought a leg of lamb especially."

Cliff emerged from the gloom of the hurricane lamps which lit small areas of bitten and scraped clay banks. He waited until the footsteps of his wife climbed out of earshot, and he said disapprovingly, "She prefers it up there to down here."

At the far end of the basement there was a bed, some expensive electronic gadgetry, a table, and a chair with a stiff back. Along one wall were plastic clothes baskets piled high with back copies of *Albania Today* and summarised news bulletins from Tirana published in English for the foreign readership.

But back at the door Cliff was studying my feet. He said I might like to pull on a pair of house slippers, or jandals. There was a pile of them at the door. I would be much more comfortable, he said, and in such a way as to suggest that non-compliance carried the weight of a cultural slight.

He found me a worn pair of green jandals. "There," he said, happy.

"Chai?" And he busied himself with lighting a Bunsen burner. "Go ahead. Look around."

On his table was a copy of the *DX Times*. He had underlined some references to himself in the editor's chatty "Mailbag" column. "Cliff, we're getting around this month . . . From up in the tropics Cliff has heard from one he describes as Vientiane and the Voice of Afghan 17540 . . . Some really unusual ones here, Cliff. Nice work. Ed." Another section, "Shortwave Bandwatch," listed the reception details sent in by league members—the kilohertz, the country and programme: 3385, Papua New Guinea, East New Britain, "drumming and singing . . ."; Papua New Guinea, New Ireland, "Linda Ronstadt singing . . ."; Dubai, "the war in the Gulf and light music . . ."

Cliff glanced at his watch. "Right now," he said, "Radio Tirana should be broadcasting to Africa." He poured the tea, then he reached over to his dials. A moment later came the familiar static cloudburst. Then, Tirana . . .

Later, when I surfaced from this world, I was greeted with the rolling calm of Kansas Street, its tidy space and tripwire fences. Islands of tall maize grew wild around the fence posts where the mowers couldn't get close enough, and it occurred to me, not for the first time, that here in the South Pacific were bits and pieces of another world poking through, a piece of the prairie that had taken seed from our imagination.

5

The few things I knew about Albania then I had gleaned almost entirely from Cliff. It was around the time of the revolution sweeping Eastern Europe that my interest re-emerged. At the tail end of the massive crowd scenes in Prague and the wintry loneliness of a broken East German Party leader walking in the woods of a Russian asylum came the grainy blue television pictures of a street mob in Tirana.

I moved forward to the edge of my armchair as one of the mob broke clear. This renegade looked like an extra in an Elia Kazan movie—ill-fitting trousers of a rough kind of denim and something like a black pea jacket and a peaked cap. A rope was tied around his waist, and as he stepped onto the statue's knees, those at the rear of the mob raised a cheer.

Now the young man stretched for the dictator's breast pocket. He took purchase and swung freely. The crowd moved involuntarily forward, but the young man was able to clinch with his legs and grab the bronze neck, to which he fastened the rope. From here the coverage jumped forward. The screen filled up with the face of a reporter, and over his shoulder, high up in the picture, groups of men were urinating over the fallen idol.

A few months later, in Rome, the first Albanians I meet are some of those figures I had seen in the photographs dragging themselves out of Durrës harbour, clambering up the sides of ships. Short, humble figures like the ones I remember from old school photographs of men in the twenties felling timber to clear away farmland. Men amused by any special attention given them.

A need for birth certificates and other documentation has brought them back to home soil, but for so large a group their silence is chastening.

The Albanian consulate is hidden behind high walls, and from via Asmaria you can't see the tall elegant trees, the sweep of lawn, or the circular drive. There is an entranceway of perhaps half a dozen steps cut from stone, but once you are inside the door the grandeur falls away and you find yourself at the threshold of another world, one which has made a virtue out of neglect.

In the gloomy hall and waiting room the light bulbs haven't been replaced and the wallpaper has started to sag out from the wall. A shabby blue cotton shift sits loosely over a couch. Four young men perch on the edge and rise nervously to their feet whenever consulate officials in overcoats make brief appearances. It starts out orderly, but the moment pieces of paper are produced, everyone begins talking at once and the officials simply don't want to know about it. They wave their arms and retreat behind closed doors, and there they remain until the consulate closes at noon.

This was the case on Saturday. On Monday the halls and lobby are deserted—it's an entirely different place—and a man in a dapper suit and with polished English says, "You would like to visit Albania. Yes, why not."

Two days later, in Bari, I'm standing at the stern of a ship watching the procession of secondhand cars crammed with food and clothes and electrical appliances enter the hold.

Already we're an hour late in leaving and another dozen cars are still on the wharf. The drivers check that the ropes holding down fridges and televisions on the car roofs are secure. They can't check this enough times. The overwhelming concern is for practicality, which is the kind of thing Cliff would warm to. For the first time on this trip I can actually place him. One driver has removed his shoes and another driver is examining their heels. Cliff would have an opinion on such things.

Just two cars left now. An announcement that the bar has opened clears the decks. A little later the ship gives a shudder, and down on the wharf three Italian officials in black uniforms rock back on their heels with the satisfaction of a difficult job at an end. There are no other farewells. I stay out there until one by one the lights go out along the Italian coast.

In the night something like a cold hand touched my cheek and I felt Albania reach out—a cold puff of wind sent down from those tan-coloured mountain peaks which, for a moment, I can't think where or how they have come to mind. Of course, I'm thinking of Syldavia from the Tintin books.

The lounge is quiet as a morgue—men in socked feet lie back with their mouths open. The ship feels like a giant crib rocking gently in the swell.

Out on deck there is a full yellow moon, and briefly, I think I have it all to myself. The next thing I see is the lit end of a cigarette, and here he comes, a lone figure shuffling from the doorway of the saloon. He takes a few steps and stops, to hold his position against the pitch and roll of the ship; then he sets off again.

He stops short of me with his pissed-pants stance. "Allemagne?" Then he tries something in Italian which I fail to pick up. He shakes his head, and in perfect English he says, "I asked if you were Russian."

His name is Mister Jin, although this comes later.

I tell him I am visiting Albania.

"Well yes," he says. "We all are. This is where the ship is destined, surely. But you are not Albanian." Then he asks that I forgive his rudeness, but he is unaccustomed to such a phenomenon. "Why would anyone visit Albania?" he wonders. "Perhaps you are a spy? In Albania there is hardly anyone who isn't a spy."

He waits to see what I think of that—instead, I congratulate him on his English. And he laughs loudly and heartily, a laugh which smells strongly of alcohol.

"Allow me," he says, "to introduce you to one of my closest friends . . ." From the inside of his coat he produces a bottle of Greek brandy.

He is returning home from visiting his son in Italy, and this being his first time abroad, I am curious to hear his impressions. Was it everything he had expected? But he answers by saying his son is very happy there.

"His life is very satisfactory. Very satisfactory," he says.

We drink to that, and Mister Jin suddenly begins to sing.

"Row, row, row your boat
Gently down the stream . . ."

He asks if I know this particular English song.

Then, with passable sincerity, he says he has one or two questions on his mind. There are some things he would like to know about my country.

"Did you fight against the Nazis in the war?"

"Do you possess the grape—and grow corn?"

"Is it a prime minister or a king that you have?"

"Do you have black people?"

"It is coming into summer there, I believe. Do you like to swim? My personal preference is to frogkick."

"Oh dear," he says merrily. He checks himself. "That is also an English colloquialism, yes, this is a fact? Good, I am satisfied."

"So why, my friend, what has brought you to Albania?

"Ah, you are a writer. This is good. This is very good indeed.

"Ismail Kadare. You know him? Excellent. But you must read Dossier H. To understand the tragedy of my country this is the book."

"I'll look out for it."

"Ah, but naturally you will not find it in English. So I will tell you.

"First," he says, "you must understand. Information and genealogy are everything in Albania. Under Hoxha there was no other reality. You understand?

"Under Hoxha, everyone had to write out their biografi. Each year it was to be updated and added to—information such as: Have you been turned down by the Party? Was your father a partisan? Were your grandparents Zogists? Or collaborators? Your biografi would tell.

"The story Kadare wrote was of two Englishmen who have come to Albania to research an academic work on Homer. Our secret police are immediately suspicious. Who is this person Homer? What does he want? Is he a collaborator? A foreign agent? We must find out. So, a *sigourimi* is sent to spy on the Englishmen. He eavesdrops. He learns the questions the Englishmen ask. And eventually a dossier emerges on this foreign agent . . . this saboteur called Homer. You understand?"

I mention my interest in Hoxha, although the word I use is "dictator" and Mister Jin reacts with mock surprise.

" 'Dictator,' you say. 'Great Leader,' we said."

Enver Hoxha, he continues, had been a religion.

"Even I. I was very, very sad when Enver died. At my office no one was brave enough to mention his death. We didn't dare speak for what might come out. This is a fact. Imagine, please, if we said the Emperor was dead and he turned out not to be? We waited for the radio report before we could speak of his death. Some had cried with genuine grief, others cried because they thought it dangerous not to. Some turned white believing something catastrophic would happen. The crops would shrivel and die. The seas would rise. They would be obliged to walk on stilts.

"My friend," he says, "you cannot imagine."

In the distance four small lights pin down a charcoal-smudged horizon. Then, around dawn, Albania begins to emerge from something more than hearsay. The notion of clouds gives way to layers of hill; their tops are darkly pencilled and fold back on one another. An hour later, as we enter the port of Durrës, Mister Jin is still at my side. The rest of the passengers have come out on deck. They stand shoulder to shoulder, silent for the most part, and with a kind of shortsightedness that insists landfall is still half a mile off.

And there, high on the hill overlooking the town, is King Zog's Palace from one of Cliff's photographs.

We nudge the wharf and a stern rope is played out. An orderly crowd waits down on the wharf. A single hand is raised—and because it is so utterly alone, there is something almost defiant about it. And it occurs to me that Albanians are probably unaccustomed to welcoming back their own. Young soldiers shoulder rifles. Faces peer down from the upper floors of a grimy yellow building which is located almost ludicrously, as if it intends to meet visiting ships on equal terms. Its upper windows are missing and some of the floors lack walls. The building is a mouthful of broken teeth.

Standing in the rubble are thin, watchful men, unshaven, lank-haired with sideburns, dressed in bell-bottoms. It must have rained a short time earlier. Puddles and grime fetch away in the distance to a ramshackle customs house. Beyond this, a long stretch of rolled barbed wire separates the street from the wharf area, and hemmed in behind, hundreds and hundreds of people stand in the cold and mud, "waiting," as it is often said of the fishermen in Durrës during winter, according to Mister Jin, "for the sea to freeze over so they can walk to Italy."

I remember Cliff's parting advice to take American money, to keep it in small denominations and spread it throughout my person. I should put bank notes in my socks, but not in my shoes. Pack Elastoplast and anti-bacterial powder. Always travel with a bottle of raki. In the event of a holdup offer the bandits a drink, and try to be lighthearted.

I stick to Mister Jin's side through customs, shadow him through the gap in the barbed wire. With widening eyes the crowd stares back. They press their hands against the wire. No doubt they have questions of their own. For the moment it is not Cliff's bandits that I see in these people but something rather more frightening about a crowd that has lost its tongue.

We get to the railway station ahead of the other passengers off the boat. I have a small confession to make. I tell Mister Jin that I have come here with notions of Greece. I had imagined blue skies and small villages carved out of whitewash.

Mister Jin returns a puzzled look. He asks, "Where is this place, please?"

We sit in a carriage blackened from fire. Glass crunches under our feet. A cold draught is blowing through the shattered windows. On the outskirts of Durrës bits of land float on lakes. Feet dangle over the sides of walls with water below. We leave the last of the wet washing hung out over balconies. Then we are in the countryside. A horse strains to pull a cart through a field of ploughed mud. In the distance an old woman ankle-deep in mud is buckled under a load of wood.

"What a shame it is," says Mister Jin, "that you have chosen to come here in winter."

So far Albania is bog, or under water, washed out in colour, and its bare hills are without ski lifts. The depletedness of the view from the train window is only marginally relieved by our arrival at Tirana. Although we seem to have come upon it too suddenly. One moment we are in the countryside—the next, gliding by at train speed are grey slabs of apartments and there is no time to compare the gradual approach to Tirana with American writer Rose

Wilder Lane's description of sixty years earlier: "You must come over the mountains from Durazzo and see at the foot of the mountains—with old Dajti stretched like some prehistoric monster against the sky above it—the long stretch of trees that's Tirana and the white minarets rising."

By the time a German journalist, Harry Hamm, arrived in Albania, thirty years after Rose Wilder Lane, of the country's 530 mosques only a dozen remained. Some had been turned into theatres, others into gymnasiums. The Orthodox church on the hill at the southern edge of Tirana, he noted, had been turned into a restaurant and the altar into a counter on which a chromium-plated coffee machine displayed a "latest social achievement" plaque.

From the railway station we walk through the city to the Dajti Hotel, its namesake looming over the city as Rose Wilder Lane described, but its summit covered in grey mist. Every visitor mentions Dajti, but now I can see why. Tirana feels like rubble at the bottom of a cliff.

By the time we reach Skanderbeg Square, the mist has turned to rain.

"Such a pity," says Mister Jin, and he reminds me: in summer a cradle of smiles dangles over Tirana.

"Where are the birds?" I ask.

"Birds?"

It has just occurred to me. It has to do with the absence of traffic, the total absence of noise, I am sure, otherwise I would not have thought of birds.

"The birds are surely in the trees," he says.

We come onto Skanderbeg Square, which is vast and rain-soaked. We stop to look at the pedestal where the statue of Enver Hoxha had stood, and which is now occupied by small children. One boy strikes a pose and pops a muscle. A soldier posted there heaves his rifle and looks off in another direction.

From the square we follow the edge of a park. Mister Jin says we are nearly there.

"Okay. Okay," call some small boys crouched by the fires of a chestnut vendor.

A young man selling newspapers calls out pleasantly, "Bush!" He raises the Democrat salute. Two fingers.

I feel as if I'm the only foreigner in Tirana. A special emissary of some kind.

In fact the Dajti, as I discover, is full of UN people and logistics experts from Western relief agencies. The other guests are visiting "businessmen." Romanian, Italian, Hungarian—they are all here. The foyer of the Dajti is a kind of piazza. The noise missing in the square is in the hotel. In the days ahead the visiting "businessmen" fail to shed their heavy coats or venture beyond the smoke-filled lobby. At night they resettle in the lounge and sit at the low coffee tables under a thickening cloud of smoke. They raise their glasses, propose toasts, and talk of "opportunities," while a woman in a leopardskin coat goes from one man's knee to another's.

In the foyer of the Dajti, I begin to thank Mister Jin, until he stops me.

"But you are a guest in my country. It has only been a short time together, but I feel secure to think of us as friends."

He places both his hands on my shoulders. His unshaven cheeks brush with mine.

At the door he calls back: "Dossier H! Don't forget."

6

I had to wait another four days before meeting Gert Munz. He'd been on a home visit to Wiesbaden. His wife refuses to live in Tirana—and Tirana, of course, offers nothing for his teenage children. Munz was a career diplomat and Tirana was his posting.

"What am I to do? I am held hostage." He smiled agreeably.

I liked and trusted his wrinkly eyes. A wild idea brought out a twinkle and then he might begin, "You know, I have an idea . . ." But there were unguarded moments too, such as when I came upon him waiting for me down in the hotel foyer lost in thought, that I imagined him preoccupied with crossing out the days, weeks, and months he had left in Tirana.

While he wished me well he was less than confident of my finding Shapallo.

"It is possible. Of course. But . . ." There, his worst fears ended the possibility, and he shook his head.

Munz felt a considerable sympathy for Shapallo and had worked hard to organise a title de voyage. In their short time together they appear to have grown quite fond of each other. Shapallo enjoyed backgammon and their evenings were spent over Munz's board. They drank down a bottle of Port and Shapallo spoke of his future, of what it might hold for him. His wishes were simple enough, as Munz recalled: "To eat a freshly caught fish and to sit in a public square with his face turned up to the sun."

The ferry *Appia* had duly arrived from Venice and the time came to shift the first thousand refugees from the besieged embassies to Durrës and onto Brindisi. The regime in its paranoia insisted the transfer be carried out at night, and Munz had watched the vehicle rumble off down Embassy Row and Shapallo lean out the open end of the truck to wave farewell.

But something had happened along the way. Shapallo had failed to turn up in Durrës—somewhere along the thirty-kilometre journey, Munz seemed to think, the refugees had tipped Shapallo from the truck.

"Where is he now? I have no idea. Is he even alive? Frankly, I think not."

Then he added, "Where would a man like that hide?"

One afternoon I waited for Munz on the steps of the Palace of Culture, reading the graffiti cribbed from the comics and music sent home from the first wave of boat refugees: "GOD CREATED HARLEY DAVIDSON . . . FUCK YOU SISTERS . . . METALLICA FOR ALL . . . REIGN IN BLOOD."

Above the graffiti the green blinds blew out the broken windows, catching on the shards of glass. A gentle rain began to fall and a sea of black umbrellas went up around the square. The umbrellas scattered as an erratically driven Fiat —another trophy sent home by refugees—careered through the crowd in the square. I tried to imagine the sound of bicycle tyres on wet asphalt, a city of bicycles and pedestrians that had once been Tirana.

The city was little more than a bazaar when Joseph Swire, an English traveller, passed through in the thirties: "There were no new buildings and Tirana seemed decrepit, muddy, grey for want of the sun which lagged behind heavy clouds."

Italian money, influence, and eventual occupation went some way towards raising the city above open sewers and small cottages cobbled from baked mud and boulders. The new style, in fact, was uncompromisingly Italian. Civic pride rebounded along the "great double-barrelled Boulevard Mussolini," eventually to become Boulevard Stalin and, in 1991, Boulevard of the Martyrs.

The Italians had built the government ministries—four-storey-high pastel-coloured buildings. Behind these they had constructed pretty villas with patios and gardens enclosed by high walls.

The villas had eventually fallen into the hands of the Party of Labour and been cordoned off.

The "block" is what Munz had wanted to show me. It is less than five minutes' walk from the Palace of Culture, and yet, despite its central location, the block had been successfully sealed off by soldiers and hidden cameras to share with the outside world a kind of quarantine status. While it had been acceptable to acknowledge that the block and the outside world existed, the line was drawn at actually experiencing or talking about either. Those who were permitted to "venture out" were ordered not to speak to anyone of what they had seen. It was better for everyone concerned that they simply pretend to have seen and heard nothing. That way everyone would be happier. Eventually the details of their journey would wear off like a lapsed dream, and in time, ventured Munz, the traveller might begin to doubt that he had even made the journey. When you reached this level of deception the traveller was rewarded with officialdom's kindly smiles.

Comrade.

Two months earlier the block had been opened to the public for the first time. During the first weeks families had wandered arm in arm through leafy streets in a kind of vacation spirit. People spoke of Paris. Vienna. Rome. They were not quite sure what to make of the block, it being quite unlike anything else in their own country. The thing that had struck people most was how the air changed.

And it was true! In the space of a few blocks it was as if we had travelled from East to West. We had left behind the shabbiness and mud of Tirana's unfinished pavements for quiet, tree-lined streets and sealed pavements. The water-stained apartment houses had given way to stylish villas. There were patios and gardens with luxuriant foliage trained to spill over high walls.

We walked beneath other walls topped with barbed wire and broken glass. Munz pointed to the cap of a soldier standing in the garden. A little further on, it was possible to see the soldier's green tunic through the last of the yellowing grapevines.

Opposite a small park of tall poplars stood the Hoxha compound—a three-storey block which sprawled in the manner of a collapsed cake. In style it owed something to the model homes featured in editions of the *Ladies' Home*

Journal from the 1950s—here and there a stolid brick façade conceded a pink shutter. Climbing rose grew over a black iron railing. At the bottom of the garden stood a sculpture of a shepherd playing his flute to a herd of goats.

At the other end of the property were greenhouses with mandarin trees. Standing guard here were two soldiers. Munz called them over to the fence.

The soldiers' rifle butts were carved with initials. Poor nutrition had scarred their faces with acne, and any authority they were capable of was undermined by red blemishes and bewildered eyes.

When Munz asked them what they were doing, the soldiers consulted each other. They shrugged, and then the younger one, with a sheepish, apologetic smile, mentioned the possibility of riots. He pointed to the greenhouses behind, still intact.

We crossed the street to the park. From here we had an uninterrupted view up the rruga running the length of the Hoxha compound. On the corner closest, one of the country's new entrepreneurs had set himself up with a pair of bathroom scales. A cardboard sign invited customers to weigh themselves for two lek.

"It is as you can see," said Munz. "A hopeless situation."

Shapallo had lived in the block, but Munz didn't know where. The dentist had described a small sunken garden surrounded by high walls. He couldn't see out, and people couldn't see in. In fact, he'd had no idea of his street address since he received no mail and took no telephone calls. Munz seemed to think that the windows in the villa had been shuttered all year round.

From what he had told Munz, Shapallo had lived for nearly twenty years in a comfortable cage. He also said that on the night of Hoxha's death the cage door had deliberately been left open, and he had fled the block for the countryside, travelling at night and sleeping by day in concrete bunkers.

On the train from Durrës I had seen the bunkers squatting on the roadside and perched in fields of tilled earth. They were positioned to shoot the enemy coming over the rise. South of Durrës I had seen them sitting on the beaches like mutant grey jellyfish, watching the horizon.

After years of "soft living" Shapallo had suddenly found himself foraging to survive. For a time he had subsisted on chestnuts and olives. Moving down the coast towards Sarandë, he had described to Munz his wandering through the orange-scented groves, picking fruit off the ground, a man with a straight back who placed each foot delicately, as if trying to tiptoe away from his shadow.

7

Each morning the student interpreters gather outside the Dajti to pick up casual work from the foreigners. As soon as I appear they look off in another direction or scuff their shoes on the concrete steps. We have given up on each other—at least this is what I tell the crowd in the hotel bar at night. Oddly enough it tends to be in the bar, here among foreigners, that Albania draws closer and seems more real than the city I wander through by day. The murals in the state shops offer loaves of bread, meat, vegetables; the walls drip with fruit, while the shelves collect dust. All the blame, I'm told, rests with the countryside, where the peasants forgot to sow last spring. It's the countryside I hear about in the Dajti bar each night.

Another food warehouse looted and set on fire. Elsewhere a truck carrying relief stores has been hijacked. In a small isolated village up near the Montenegrin border the people are angry. They want to know why only selected families are receiving food and clothing. How can one family be more deserving than the next when the fact is everybody is starving? And in the third incident of its kind, bandits have stolen the new beds from a hospital in the northern city of Shkodër. One agency run by the French is pulling out. They have had a gutsful. The country can go and knock on the door of hell.

Hey, this is not the Sudan, they say. It's worse. The army can't be trusted to guard the convoys. In the mountain villages the infant mortality rate is up there with that of the African disaster areas.

In the bar I hear about another country. For the hundredth time I'm told that I cannot imagine. This time it is Bill Foster, a tall, stoop-shouldered Midwesterner with unblinking eyes, on Albania's "African mortality rates." It is a sobering subject. We stare into our glasses until Bill relieves the gloom. "This is what I say to Sharon when she asks me what it's like here. 'It's like, hey, Sharon, put on your best coat and shoes and climb into the cattle truck. It's Saturday night. We're going off into town.' "

We laugh. Some of us ponder "Sharon." Some of us don't quite believe in her. Bill's talk of Sharon has the same uneasy effect as the name "Shapallo" has on the student interpreters.

Bill is headed north in the morning. He says I'm welcome to make the trip. Everyone has been saying Shkodër's the place. Politically, Shkodër is "hot." I actually have other reasons for visiting Shkodër.

There will be a small detour to the northeast—if I can handle that, he says. There are some warehouses to inspect. But from Kukës, Shkodër is a five- or six-hour run.

We leave early the next morning. There are five of us: Teti, the driver; Anila, Bill's interpreter; and a pretty, soft-faced girl whose name I fail to catch. Bill introduces her as the "economist."

"Doesn't mean shit, though. Half the population is a director of something, and when you look them up they're working in a tin shed with a hole in the roof.

"It's okay," he says. "She can't speak English."

The economist rides in the back with me. Bill rides shotgun. He has virtually nailed himself to the side of Teti, who's there because every relief vehicle is required to employ a local driver.

Children with small grimy faces rush fearlessly out to the middle of the road. Until a year ago they had to worry only about the horse-drawn carts, bicycles, and the occasional bus or truck. But now the kids spot the Aid insignia on the side of the Land Cruiser and try to touch its sides.

We pass through a bleak landscape of malnourishment, listening to Teti's pirated tapes of Steely Dan, Sting, and the

New Kids on the Block. Through the windshield Albania shifts to plain vista. We pass through it in our capsule of warm air conditioning and nice upholstery. We are sufficiently removed from what we see. Those small kids out there rushing out to the road, that wide mouth yelling for gum, is something I might have seen in the pages of *National Geographic*. Bill says the Yugoslav truck drivers started this thing of throwing gum from their window and now in every town we pass through kids sit on the road like birds after a downpour.

I'm happy to be getting outside Tirana at last, just to escape the rain. I thank Bill for this lift and he waves his pipe. "Hey," he says. He can use the company.

Two days ago he had taken a couple of London *Daily Mirror* reporters out to a food drop. After a while, it had become obvious to Bill that Harry, the photographer, was doing a "Girls of Albania thing."

"Every halfway decent gal we stopped for so Harry could do his thing. One place there was this very pretty gal washing clothes in a ditch. I said to Harry, you know, half-joking, 'Harry, do you want me to go and splash a little water on her shirt . . . You know, for a wet T-shirt shot?' "

We laugh—and Anila pulls her cheap fur coat around her shoulders a little more. She speaks only when spoken to—but the soft-faced economist doesn't speak at all. Bill offered her a barley sugar and back came the most beautiful smile. Bill says it's just a "language thing." But later I do hear him ask Anila whether the economist is okay.

We are in the countryside now. Circles of men squat at the roadside. Others hack away at stumps for firewood. A blackened smokestack rises in the distance and a few minutes later we pass a chemical and metallurgy plant. Even from the car window it appears eccentric and ungainly, as if the regime had followed the advice of a young child using Meccano for the very first time.

The rust-coloured King Zog bridge takes us across the vast shingle flats of the Mat River. Here, the road starts to climb inland until we are high above the river valley. A convoy of Italian trucks piled high with grain passes us coming the other way. As each truck goes by, Teti takes his hand off the wheel to give the Democrat salute. The Italians show no interest—they stare through Teti to the road ahead, an imaginary road paved all the way home to Italy. The same stony indifference had sat with the Italian drivers in Durrës as they lined their trucks up beneath a grain chute. The Italians wore red, white, and blue neckerchiefs. In their khaki uniforms and high-laced boots they could have stepped out of an L.A. nightclub. I think it was in the bar of the Dajti that somebody told me the Italian army uniform was designed by Armani.

We continue to climb this narrow road. Either side of the ravine the slopes of loose rock rise to blue sky, the first I have seen since arriving in the country. On the ridgetops the trees are changing colour and there is a lovely suffusion of oranges and yellows. I ask Bill if he knows the names of the trees. He asks Anila. Her shoulders rise and fall. She asks the economist. She doesn't know. No one knows.

On a visit to Burgeget, King Zog's village in the Mati Valley, Swire describes soft hills well grown with mulberry, walnut, cherry, and chestnut trees.

We enter a loop in the road, and as we draw around the last bend, melted into a pinnacle of rock up ahead is an old

Greek Orthodox church. Its roof suddenly catches sunlight, and as the road travels underneath this splash of gold we enter Rubik.

In the space of a bend the road dissolves to a market-place and Teti snarls at everything in our path. Oxen, gum-worshipping kids, horse-drawn carts. He leans on the horn, and people stop their conversations to stare at us.

"Teti! Anila, will you tell him to stop that bullshit . . ."

And again: "Don't piss these people off, Teti. Leave the friggin' horn."

A rock bounces off the side of the Land Cruiser and that does it. We lurch to a halt. Teti is out the door and running back up the road.

Bill just refuses to look. He says to Anila, "He's a friggin' idiot. I want you to tell him that, okay."

In the back window I see Teti catch up with a kid and start to smack him about the head.

Bill says, "What's he doing? Tell me what the hell he is doing. I'm not going to look, but I need to know."

The economist continues to sit with her arms folded and an imperturbable gaze aimed at her side window. Anila turns around in her seat. She reports to Bill: "Teti is coming back. He's let the boy go."

Flushed and stiff with dignity, Teti settles in behind the wheel. Bill doesn't budge a whisker. He takes a deep breath; then he says quietly to Anila, "Go ahead. Tell him."

So Anila says something to Teti, who ignores it. He starts up the Land Cruiser and we are on our way.

"Tell him, Anila . . . One month ago with Kemal . . ." Bill turns around to explain with his pipe. "Kemal, you know

... the same make as Teti, as all this macho bullshit. The same thing happened in a little town north of here. Rock hits the side of the van. Kemal stops. Marches back to deal with some farm boys and gets his ass kicked.

"Hey!" he says to Anila. "Remind Teti about Kemal . . . His arm was all mangled . . . half his friggin' teeth left on the roadside!"

Bill meditates for a few more kilometres. Then he says to Anila, "Tell him if he ever does that again I'm throwing him out."

Anila says something and Teti's ears turn red.

We cross the Mat River again and catch sight on the far hillside above the railway line of a huge painted slogan: "July is the month of working hard."

Near Rrëshen we check out a food warehouse guarded by a man with an old hunting rifle. He and Bill embrace warmly. Bill gives the man some tobacco. He takes a quick peep in the windows of the warehouse, and then we continue on into Rrëshen.

The road into the town climbs a hill, and on the side overlooking the valley is a striking bronze sculpture of four women—one woman shoulders a rifle, another carries a book, the third a pick. The hand of the fourth woman points to the road ahead. Anila says the sculpture represents the "struggle against obscurantism."

"The women have returned from working on the railway construction. In other words," she says, "they show the correct path."

The other reason for visiting Rrëshen is that Anila married a pharmacist from here. We stop by the pharmacy. It is open but has no drugs. Anila's husband has gone to Italy to work as a labourer for a few months and a letter is waiting for her at the pharmacy. She goes off to read it alone at the foot of the bronze women. Bill tells Teti to stay with the vehicle. He's not to drive it—nor is he to leave it.

He stays parked outside the Town Hall with an Albanian version of *Jesus Christ Superstar* cranked up while Bill and I go to look for some food. The one café has its chairs stacked up on the tables. It quickly transpires that there is nothing left to eat in Rrëshen, and as we come out of the café a small crowd greets us with looks of amusement. It is all good-natured. Bill seems to think they are apologising for the state of things. One of the elders steps forward, but before he can explain anything Teti guns the Land Cruiser across the square and suddenly the crowd are scattered like pigeons.

"Teti!" For a moment I think Bill is going to throw his pipe at the grinning face in the windshield. Instead, he says to me, "This is supposed to be a favour. We employ the local people. But I get a madman."

Teti hangs out the window waiting for Bill's instructions, the motor drumming.

"Jesus. Just go and get Anila."

"Anila . . . Okay!"

And Teti's foot falls upon the accelerator with renewed purpose as Bill finishes: "We've gotta apologise to these people."

We drive on for another hour, climbing and twisting through high hill country. We have gone back far enough now that the leaves of the chestnut trees lie on the ground, leaving the branches looking lonely and stark. One time we stop so Teti can relieve himself and in the silence we hear the bells of a goatherd ring down from the hillsides.

A few months earlier Bill had visited a village so remote that he was the first foreigner the inhabitants had seen since the war. On that occasion the villagers had seen a British parachutist float down from the sky. He was taken in by a local priest and a month later smuggled out of Albania. Fifty years later Bill drove into the village and had a wonderful lunch there.

"Great bread, yogurt, raki, and this wonderful antipasto kind of thing, you know? A bit of red pepper and onion . . ." He smiles over the stem of his pipe at the memory and we all fall silent with hunger.

"It was a blast, a couple of hundred people sitting around staring at us for a couple of hours."

Bill says he knows of a "trucker's stop" near here. It is in a place called "the neck of the mountain," an accurate-enough description for where the road doubles back on itself. Bill's "trucker's stop" turns out to be a small grotto of roofing iron and rocks stacked on one another. We arrive at the same time as a truckload of young soldiers but manage to scramble in ahead.

The proprietor, a small wizened man, ladles the runny white yogurt into greasy plastic bowls and slaps them down on a crude wooden bench. Then the soldiers start to pour in and soon we are standing shoulder to shoulder in crowded silence—jammed inside this smoky grotto with these poor half-starved boys in green tunics.

We grind on to Kukës in low gear for another hour. Bill has given up directing Teti—and despite the driver's assurances, "I'm okay, I'm okay," Bill just grabs the wheel whenever the moment requires intervention to pull us onto the shoulder again. Teti feeds in a tape of The Who's rock opera Tommy. Bill turns it down. Teti sneaks the dials up. And on it goes.

We stop one more time when Anila feels carsick. It is deadly quiet. The road trickles invitingly up to a rise.

When I asked Cliff how he had got around he said, "Train. Bus. Foot." And in my more fanciful moments I imagined myself doing as Joseph Swire had done, walking between villages with a burro and usually with armed escorts.

Bill says, "Go ahead. Stretch out your ligaments. We'll be by in twenty minutes."

At one point I hear Anila violently heave, and when I look back there is Bill sitting on a rock, knees crossed, lighting his pipe.

Another ten minutes and I'm at the pass gazing across the tops of gold and black hills which roll on to Macedonia in the east and, to the north, Montenegro. Small boys minding goats above the roadside whistle out from the scrub.

8

POPULI PARTI ENVER, just as it appears on the postage stamps, is emblazoned on the hillside above Kukës.

Twenty years ago the workers at the copper smelter had

collected small stones on the hillside and carefully arranged the stones to spell the slogan.

I learnt this from Mustaph, an unemployed journalist, who looks after the food distribution in Kukës.

Mustaph had been waiting on the hotel steps for our arrival. A man of about fifty, round-headed, with greying temples and quick, intelligent eyes, and formidably sober. His overcoat was the one he had bought in Leningrad after being sent there to study literature and languages in the fifties.

I think he found my questions about POPULI PARTI ENVER a little tiresome. The slogan bore down on the town in such a way as to suggest a major landmark; but as Mustaph's uncooperative silence seemed to suggest, a landmark not inquired of but accepted as readily as the clouds and hilltops and other natural phenomena. POPULI PARTI ENVER could be seen from anywhere in Kukës—a "new city" of bleak housing blocks. The old town lay beneath the new lake in a valley which had been flooded for hydroelectric purposes. The hydroelectric plant was a happier subject for Mustaph.

Work on the modern city had started in the sixties. People living down in the old town on the valley floor could gaze up to the cloudline and watch their future homes going up. They were promised playgrounds and hospitals, and in the evenings, Mustaph said, the old people would sit in their gardens and watch the last of the summer evening depart the concrete shells up there on the rise.

One day in the seventies the people had all trooped up to the new town and where the new hospital was sited a park bench had been built for the elderly to sit and watch the water level rise below. It had taken months, years. First the streets turned a muddy colour, then the water rushed inside the small stone houses and rose up the walls until there were just rooftops to gaze upon like floating islands or garden stepping-stones across a lake. Finally the "stepping-stones" had disappeared altogether, and now, looking upon the lake, I found it hard to believe that another city, with its quarrels, blood feuds, and arranged marriages, lay beneath this calm blue surface.

We booked into the hotel with a view of the lake. Anila went to bed. Teti was given the rest of the afternoon off. And with the economist and Mustaph giving directions we set off for the warehouse.

Somewhere on our way through a housing estate a rock bounces off the side of the Land Cruiser. Bill hardly raises a hair.

"Kids. Same the world over," he says, and Mustaph is relieved to hear this.

The "industrial zone" is on the other side of town and we are there in another five minutes. A woman in a blue cotton smock unchains the gates, and as we drive to the end of a yard we are chased by a crowd of gaunt figures in cotton and flapping canvas shoes. The moment we park, their faces press up to the window.

"Looking for gum, betcha," says Bill, and quickly forgets them. He's busy fiddling with a tape. "What the hell has Teti done here . . ." But then the deck receives the tape, and Bill sits back with relief. "Sharon put me on to this," he says.

Bill removes his pipe. His eyelids close, to Patsy Cline.

A pane of glass separates him from an old man whose toothless gums are barking something at the side of Bill's deaf ear. When I check with Mustaph about what the man is saying, his face creases into a smile. "He is saying, 'Show me where the war is, I want to fight.' "

I head off with Mustaph to find the person with the keys to the warehouse.

Inside a loading bay we push through a door to a smoke-filled chamber. Four women who have been crouching around an open fire and warming their hands spring to their feet and cover their faces in giggling shame. Two of the younger ones run past us for the door. Mustaph smiles tolerantly.

Across the yard the crowd is still pressed around the Land Cruiser and in the window I can make out Bill smoking his pipe, his head marking time, ever so.

We have a wait on our hands until the person with the keys to the warehouse shows. Despite the cold, Mustaph refuses to wait inside the vehicle, but stands in the yard with his hands in his coat pockets, determined to deny the cold —as if one thing has to do with admitting to the ruin surrounding us.

There's nothing to do but walk to keep warm. I head off back along the road that brought us here. Old Russian trucks and mutant vehicles with Chinese and North Korean markings—the chattel of Albania's failed marriages—splash through the puddles. Barrier gates with gaping holes wear heavy padlocks. Men huddle around in small groups.

No one has anything to do. People have turned up to

work out of habit. They watch me approach. They eye me, watchful as sheepdogs, and as I pass, in unison they call out, "May your life be long." The smokestacks look like some wasted experiment. There is no noise other than the wind off the stony walls of the valley. Opposite the "official mechanical plant of Kukës" I wander through a field full of concrete pillboxes. Their gunholes stare accusingly at the mountains. I suppose if you gaze at such things long enough you just might begin to sense the enemy on his way, if not today, then just around the next bend, in the next valley, beyond that peak. Tomorrow he will come through the mountains to learn the secret of Albania's success. "Above our homeland," the inscription reads, "we have everything . . . and that is freedom and independence."

I soon find the playground promised the inhabitants of old Kukës. It had started out as a reasonably bold idea before foundering along the way—for lack of either materials or the will to take it any further. The playground bomb shelter has made it through to completion, likewise a white cement sculpture of a mother cradling a child.

The sculptured mother cradles her child a short distance from a rusted Ferris wheel that has seized up. Surrounding it is a mangle of steel, from which small children in cotton clothing and bare feet swing from the makeshift bars. The children barely make a sound. I wonder if they know they are just seven hours' ferry ride from Italy.

A hand suddenly rests on my shoulder and there is Mustaph, with his clever smile.

That night in the hotel bar Bill and I got a little drunk on raki and Bill talked about Sharon. They had met while out jogging. This was in Washington. They jogged the same route, although in opposite directions. "Oh, she was real cute. She'd smile and I'd say, 'Hi.' Then we'd run off, with both of us kinda looking back over our shoulder." One morning Bill just turned around and ran with her, and he moved into her house soon after. He felt around in his jacket.

"Goddamn," he said. The photo was back in Tirana. So I showed Bill my postage stamp of Enver Hoxha—it being the only likeness I had of Shapallo. Then I told Bill about the playground, where Mustaph had surprised me. On the way back to the warehouse Mustaph had chatted away amiably. He said he had met the Great Leader three times, here in Kukës.

The first time, Enver had been visiting the copper plant. It was the second time, however, while out on a walk, that Enver suddenly paused to stare at a bare hillside. Seeing his famous smiling lines tighten with disapproval, the local Party people duly took note, and the next day, when the Great Leader's eye fell upon the same spot, a tree was found growing there. Such was the warmth of Comrade Enver's smile that it appeared to enrich the earth around the sapling—an observation which Mustaph had been obliged to report in his newspaper. These magical powers set him apart, of course. Otherwise, he had seemed a nice man. They had even talked, recalled Mustaph.

"About what?"

Mustaph said the leader had reminisced about his childhood. Soon after that, work had started on the playground.

9

This is how the day had started out, with Bill's hand drawing an imaginary line. "Now, Anila, tell him to drive smoothly between fifty and sixty. A good driver makes it smooth . . .

"Anila, tell him when I was learning to drive my father used to say, 'Always assume there is an idiot around the next bend . . .' "

Several hours later it is pitch black. We're about to enter Shkodër, but no one is talking much because of a strongly shared sense that Teti's short driving career is drawing to a close.

For the past hour we have driven through the night with Teti switching his lights off and on. As another vehicle approaches he switches his lights off and we vanish into the night. Then, just as inexplicably, the lights come back on and startled faces show up on the roadside.

Bullock drivers raise hands to their faces. Horses rear up. Then it is pitch black again, terrifyingly so. The moment passes with all of us screaming at Teti before he locates the switch.

It is impossible to wean him off it. First Bill, then me —we try to tell Teti that in the West we drive with our lights on all the time. "Anila," says Bill. "For the grace of God, will you tell him he's driving a car not a friggin' lighthouse. We are not a lighthouse. Understand?"

But the worst of it comes as Teti rambunctiously sits on

his horn at a police roadblock. There is only one other vehicle in front of us, and Teti is giving the local police the hurry-up. This is when Bill's patience finally runs dry.

"Teti! I'm begging you!"

Teti says, "No problem." He jumps out the driver's side into the night and returns holding hands with a policeman.

"Everything okay," Teti says, getting in behind the wheel.

We set off again and Bill says to Anila, "Tell him that's it. It's over. Tell him only a friggin' idiot would sit on his horn at a roadblock. That's it . . . Understand?"

"I know. I know. I keep telling him," says Anila.

Bill is still furious as we enter Shkodër. He twists around in his seat. He says, "Listen to this. Teti's father was a fighter pilot, right. He crashed his plane into a hillside and died when he was forty. It's on Teti's résumé. It's some kind of idiocy thing running in the family."

In a mercifully short time we pull up at the hotel. The Rozala. Bill thinks it'll be okay. He says, "Now listen, ask for the jam tart thing. If they still have it don't eat the cream.

"Anila," he says, "why don't you go in and make sure there's a room."

At first it does not look promising. Anila is discussing something with the man on the desk, who seems very reluctant.

In the end a set of keys is produced. Anila says I am lucky. Tomorrow is National Independence Day, followed by National Liberation Day, and the hotel clerk, to begin with, had tried to make out that the hotel was fully booked.

I look at the keys in my hand and then at Anila.

"Why would he say that?"

"Because," she says, in heavily accented English, "he is a friggin' idiot."

The hotel clerk offers a friendly wave and points me up the stairs. He wills me on—the way a swimmer urges another into cold water.

The foyer is large and in a bygone life it might even have had pretensions towards grandeur. But indifference has taken its toll and a shabbiness touches everything.

The clerk shouts something to a woman in a blue coat. She had been halfheartedly dragging a rag over the floor. Now she hurries after me, up the stairs. On the third floor she squeezes past me through the door to the hall and jams a light bulb in a socket hanging from the ceiling. She waits until I have worked the key in the door and then removes the light bulb.

I'm pleased to find light bulbs in my room—and running water. Everything is clean and tidy. The windows give onto an empty piazza. After Kukës the air is almost balmy. I can feel the nearness of the coast. In Shkodër, Europe does not feel so far off.

The Rozala has two dining rooms. The one for the Albanians is noisy and smoky, with white tablecloths covered in beer bottles and cigarette ash. From this dining room an unshaven man in a filthy waiter's jacket guides me by the elbow to the other dining room, which is resplendently empty but for two Greek women silently eating their supper of yogurt and bread.

The waiter brings me a bowl of yogurt. He asks me if I would like anything else. I ask him what else is on the menu. He says there is nothing left—but nevertheless awaits my response with waiterly elegance, a white towel draped over his forearm.

A few minutes later the dining-room doors swing open. A man in corduroys and a blue woven jersey rubs his hands. He looks like he has cottage pie on his mind. The other, a shorter man with thinning red hair, and generous enough to smile delightedly at the sight of me dining alone, rushes over to introduce himself.

Terry and Don both start to speak at once before catching themselves. I get the impression that this is something they do often. They laugh and exchange smiles. The one called Don says, "Don't mind, do you, old man?" And he helps himself to a chair at my table. He turns it round and leans his chest against the backrest and asks, "Been long in the country?"

"No. Not long," I say, and immediately regret it.

Because, suddenly, everything changes with that admission. A kind of forfeiting of seniority takes place whereby they talk and I listen.

British Telecom had given Don a vehicle stocked full with British Telecom jerseys to drive across Europe, down through Yugoslavia to Albania. Across the border a mountain man in just bare feet and a blue singlet had been the first Albanian recipient of a British Telecom pullover.

Don says, "It was pitiful. Just pitiful."

"Have you heard?" they chorused—and this time Don graciously gives Terry the go-ahead.

"Well, the thing is, we've heard rumours the Socialists are deliberately delaying distribution of grain until the election."

Leaning forward, Don rests his chin on the chair top.

"These are just rumours of course," he says, and he proceeds to pass on pickings from the rumour mill. The *sigourimi* has run an Aid truck off the road. An Albanian-American journalist has received threats and also survived a near thing with another car on a mountain road. Don is pretty sure this is the work of the *sigourimi*.

"Well, it's typical, isn't it?"

Terry tells me he is with Feed the Children. "Perhaps you saw the BBC clip on us? No . . . Well," he says, "we're taking over the institution for the mentally handicapped children. Roger Hamilton is coming over from the *Sunday Times*. He's going to do a piece. He really cares about it."

"Oh yeah, Roger does," says Don.

"I mean, it's not just copy. He really does care," vouches Terry. "We were going to put in windows and fix it up— but in the end we decided the mobs would only ruin it. So we're going to take the kids out and relocate them."

"Relocate them is the answer," Don says. "You have to just move in and take over."

"It's such a tragedy," says Terry. "Listen. Eat your yogurt. Don't let us hold you up. God, I would kill for sausages."

"Give me a pint of Guinness," says Don a little later. "Have you tasted the grog here? Pure horse piss. Still, food would be nice too, wouldn't it? In one village I saw a family of seven living in a single hut with two pigs and a cow. Seven! And they had only one bed and two aluminium pots between them."

Any moment one of them is going to ask, "So, what brings you here, mate?" Any moment now and I'll have to explain away my various jigsaw pieces—Cliff, Kansas, Sha-pallo, and the exiles.

I stand up to leave and Terry moves his chair back. "Well, it's been lovely," he says. I get to the door just ahead of Don's discovery: "Oi, what about your supper? You've left your yogurt."

I hurry across the foyer and bound up the stairs. Then, for godsakes, I hear footsteps hurrying after me—but it is the woman with the light bulb. She waits until my light goes on; then the hallway is plunged back into darkness.

I shut the window and slip into bed with Queen Ger-aldine's account of her marriage to Zog.

10

In 1938 Geraldine appeared on the bal-cony of a villa in Tirana, the Albanian flag fluttering behind her. When a sudden breeze wrapped the red and black col-ours around her shoulders, the crowd gathered below took this as a promising omen and roared its approval. On the day of the wedding, King Zog declared a three-day celebra-tion. Tribesmen from all over the country—the Ghegs from the north and the Tosks from the south—gathered in Tirana to witness the event. Fifty other couples who had chosen this day for their marriage gathered in Skanderbeg Square. They were all given a queen's dowry consisting of a bed, blankets, and two pillows.

Among the wedding gifts received by Zog and his new queen were four prancing white Lippizaner horses from the

Regent of Hungary—a handsome phaeton to transport the bride on her wedding day. Hitler sent a "long scarlet supercharged Mercedes with a removable roof and white leather upholstery." Mussolini gave four copper vases.

Zog was sufficiently moved to declare an amnesty for hundreds of his political enemies, many of whom had sworn to kill him after the Albanian tradition of blood feud.

Queen Geraldine cut the three-metre-wide wedding cake with the King's sabre—and later they drove to Durrës for the honeymoon. In Durrës the King gently ushered his young bride over the threshold of a marble pavilion he had built especially for her.

The King showed his bride the large reception room furnished in Louis XIV style. They "discovered" the bedroom. The King cleared his throat and left the room briefly. A maid handed Geraldine a white silk nightgown. She disappeared, and Geraldine slipped between the sheets and waited.

"Quickly and passionately Zog possessed her. Not as a king but as a proud son of the Eagles . . . His bride was no different from other virgins. No one can explain the deep personal shock and physical discomfort of a woman when she is made love to for the first time . . . [Geraldine] lay softly whimpering into her pillow as the King left her side and retired to a chaise longue at the other end of the room."

There was a moment's embarrassment in the morning. The maid was terribly upset because she had lost the Queen's nightgown. And when Geraldine put the matter to the King, Zog blushed. He said he had required the nightgown as proof of her virginity. Parliament required such proof. It was a matter of protocol and accordingly Zog had sent Geraldine's silk nightgown along to the President.

The birth of Leka I was celebrated by a military parade, the largest Albania had ever staged. As the people cheered, "Our life for the King and the Crown Prince," a squadron of Italian planes swooped low over the city and white leaflets carrying a slanderous attack on King Zog fluttered down into the streets.

It was a difficult time for Zog. Mussolini's Fascists had presented him with a list of demands—military bases were to be established on the coast and inland, the harbours and roads were to come under control of the Italian Army, and Italian interests were to be observed by revising all civil service appointments. In return, Zog could keep the throne and receive a new loan.

Two hours after rejecting the Italian demands, the Albanian Parliament decided that Zog and his Ministers must leave the country at once.

At 3 a.m. the Italians started their invasion on the coast south of Tirana, in Vlorë. Geraldine, who was still recuperating from the difficult birth of Prince Leka, had to be carried down the palace stairs on a mattress and bundled into a waiting car. So hasty was the departure that Geraldine left Tirana in only the nightgown she wore—the maid had packed her furs but overlooked the need for dresses and underwear. Geraldine and Leka sat in the back of a Chrysler. In the door the King bowed and kissed the baby on the head. To Geraldine he said, "Oh God . . . It was so short."

The next day Mussolini's son-in-law, Ciano, who had attended the wedding of Zog and Geraldine, arrived in

Tirana on a new errand. He rushed from the airport to the palace, where he made his way to the Queen's suite. When he saw the bed linen stained by afterbirth, which still lay uncollected, "Ciano kicked it across the room and, with the anger of a wild animal, howled, 'The cub has escaped!' "

In 1960, in the Bristol Hotel in Paris, Prince Leka was consecrated King before seventy representatives of Albanian groups throughout the world.

Although Leka had spent only three days on Albanian soil, he had been brought up in an Albanian household, attended to by Albanian instructors, and nurtured on the idea that he was of nobility, a prince who one day would ascend to the throne. Among the cast of "father figures" Leka's mother had enlisted General Franco, the Paraguayan strongman Alfredo Stroessner, and Pinochet.

In Spain, to which the royal family eventually moved, Leka trained his Albanian exiles for the coming guerrilla war—an idea that owed much to a morphine-induced dream of his father's. In 1961, while Leka sat by his dying father in a hospital bed in Paris, Zog's last words described the dream from which he had just awoken. He had seen Queen Geraldine, now "very old but still beautiful," standing at the prow of a ship headed for the quay at Durrës. In the same dream, Leka appeared in battle fatigues, leading a column of troops to win back the kingdom.

11

In Rome I had hoped to find an émigrés' quarter. I thought there might be a bar or a café used as a local hangout, a place where old soldiers in an alcoholic haze might create heroic homecomings. I imagined a café with a memento like the Skanderbeg flag pinned to the wall behind the bar—in the spirit of Queen Geraldine's handful of soil scooped up to remember Albania with—and riotous, drunken evenings every year Independence Day wound round.

Instead, in via Asmaria I had met Nick, an earnest student of divinity and philosophy.

Across the crowded foyer in the consulate on via Asmaria I had caught his eye, and in the clamour that broke out with the sudden emergence of a consulate official leaving his office, Nick surfaced at my side.

In a whisper he asked, "Are you English?"

He was pale and thin. A quality of a life lived indoors had rubbed off, setting him apart from his ground-grubbing compatriots.

Later, after the consulate officials had declared an end to the day's business, we had wandered out to the entrance steps.

I was full of questions. About him. The refugees. I described the café with the flag of Skanderbeg pinned to the wall. Did he know of such a place?

He glanced back to the shabby foyer and touched a finger to his lips. "Not here," he said.

We hurried off in light rain to find a trattoria.

Nick was my "first Albanian" and everything he had to say I took down. It was all new to me, and Nick's stories, which were full of intrigue, were exactly what I wanted to hear. The only disappointment was that the picturesque quarter I had hoped for did not exist. Nick gave me instead the address of a monastery belonging to an order of Franciscans.

I met him there the next day, and in a small room on the ground floor Nick explained that he had been in Rome only a few months.

The first thing he had done on his arrival was to discard his name, Ardian. A generation of youths had been named after the tribes of Illyria in a bid by the regime to trample out every shred of religious identity. Once in Rome Nick had got himself christened after Saint Nicholas.

The Franciscans were putting him up, and in exchange for board he cooked for the small order of friars. In between classes he busied himself with other menial tasks around the monastery.

Through Nick I met Friar Daniel Gjecaj, who had lived in Vatican City since fleeing the Communists in 1948. He was well into his seventies now, and the recent changes in his homeland hadn't done much to excite him.

He said, "You are going to Albania, but you won't find Albania. Only the family has survived."

He had no wish to return. Nor was he convinced by the political changes.

"Who are these people who call themselves Democrats? Where have they come from?"

He shook his head. There was nothing he had heard that gave him confidence for his country's future.

For a number of years the friar had broadcast from the "Albanie office" of Radio Vaticana. Some of these broadcasts Nick had listened to at the house of his cousin Kolec. For years Radio Vaticana had been a sworn enemy of the regime. Two or three times a week it broadcast the Pope's message, sometimes a Mass, sometimes religious instruction. Other times the friar, who was a classics scholar, spoke of the country's arts and literature, all the while grinding away to undermine the regime's creation of the "new man."

At Radio Vaticana I met Gjon Gjomarkaj, who as a small "silent, lithe" boy had waited on Joseph Swire in his father's house. The Englishman had climbed 2,000 feet above the Fani i vogel River to meet Gjon Marka Gjoni, the hereditary Chieftain of Mirditë and permanent chief of all the Catholic clans in northern Albania. Swire describes a sturdy figure in "a dark red sash holding a tobacco box and a silver mounted pistol." The pistol was a gift from Zog, who had wanted badly to get the chieftain on his government's side.

Inside the stone cottage Swire had noticed a gramophone, of all things, a gift from the Italians, who at the time considered the passes of Mirditë to be of great strategic value.

Although the boy was now a white-haired man, Swire's description still applied. The once "silent, lithe" boy had developed into a quiet, haunted man, obsessed by what he had left behind.

In 1949, as a twenty-two-year-old, he had slipped into

Greece over the Dardha Mountains near Korçë. Three times Gjomarkaj and his companions were ambushed. Gjomarkaj took bullets in his body—one bullet smashed his right leg, leaving him helpless and immobile. Fortunately for him his companions had refused his invitation to shoot him.

Gjomarkaj met me in the lobby. His prim, dark trousers and tan sports coat suggested restraint and minimal fuss. He held out a hand.

"This way, please."

On the first floor we paused admiringly before a huge colour photograph, even larger than the one of the Pope downstairs, of Radio Vaticana's transmitter towers located about twenty kilometres outside Rome.

Then Gjomarkaj held open a door into a long corridor. As far as the eye could see, signposted above each office door were the various languages of Radio Vaticana's broadcasts— Croat, Polish, Czech, Slovaccio, Ukrainian, and so on, the length of the corridor and resuming up on the next floor. Next to Lithuanie was Gjomarkaj's patch, Albanie.

"Here," he said, standing aside for me to enter his office, "here you see the free Albanie."

Gjomarkaj's scarlet flag—like the one I had imagined in the expatriates' bar—sported the black-and-gold-braided eagle. The top of his filing cabinet was dotted with smaller Albanian flags from the pre-Communist era. On the wall behind his desk was a photo of Gjomarkaj's predecessor, "an extremely provocative broadcaster" killed by Albanian agents on via del Tratone near il *Messagero* in 1976.

In this way and others, Gjomarkaj took heart that the broadcasts were getting through. And then there had been the death threats, of course. Always a good sign. But even more encouraging were the letters sent by balloon. Listeners to Radio Vaticana's Albanie Service released balloons whenever the wind blew east to west. Some, he said, had even reached Switzerland.

I could imagine Gjomarkaj's grudge quietly festering away and never letting up. Whereas, by comparison, the strength of Nick's convictions could be alarmingly volatile.

One afternoon at the monastery he told me how a chance meeting with a Dutch evangelist in the park across from the Rozala Hotel had led him to embark on a kind of blood feud against Stalin. With the friar passively looking on, Nick listed the ingredients for his home recipe for dynamite to blow up the statue of Stalin in the square of Shkodër. The Dutch evangelist had had some shattering news for Nick. He had not been baptised, and therefore, whispered the Dutchman, there could be no possibility of Nick's making it to heaven.

As he told me this, Nick's face grew more grieved. His face turned whiter than usual and his lips quivered.

"Do you not see? Hoxha tried to deny me eternal life!" he shouted. I felt him waiting for me to agree and offer solace. It was an uneasiness similar to the one I had felt when Gjomarkaj had suddenly opened the door to the Radio Vaticana chapel and watched me to see if I would cross myself.

Still, Nick had been more than helpful with names and contacts. He had fitted me out with a useful working knowledge of whom to seek out and whom to avoid. The former tended to be old priests with twenty, thirty years of prison under their belt. A sure sign in Nick's estimation of both their innocence and the strength of their conviction. He had written his family to expect me. I could hardly refuse, therefore, his request that I deliver a carton of cigarettes for his father, a radio for his younger brother, and for his mother, some Franciscan literature.

The reason I had come to Shkodër was Nick.

12

In the morning I stepped into a stinking toilet to avoid Terry and Don in the hall. I waited for their noisy departure in the lobby before coming down the stairs. It was a glorious day. Blue skies. Not quite warm. White splashes of sunlight caught patches on Taraboshi and Cukali, the mountains fringing Shkodër.

In the park opposite the Rozala, I found a new flower bed planted with shemsir bushes covering up the footprints of Lenin's statue. Stalin had gone the same way, but not without a lengthy struggle. First ropes had been tried to haul him down, then explosives. Finally it had been left to city workers to remove Stalin during the hottest part of the afternoon. I found a number of flagstones marking Stalin's old place on the piazza. The surrounding tiles looked centuries old, whereas the newer ones had a rain-swept quality.

Respect for the partisans had ensured the survival of a striking bronze sculpture on the other side of the Rozala, commemorating the "five heroes who resisted the German advance in the fields of Vigut."

From the "Heroes of Vigut" the eye travels down a wide avenue and pulls up at a pile of stones and flowers. I strolled down there, pestered by a small boy on a bike who kept on at me. "Are you a cross?"

"No," I said, something I'd never have dreamt of telling Nick.

Puzzled, the boy rode off.

The pile of stones and flowers had been placed ostentatiously, and as with the former positioning of Stalin in the piazza, there was no avoiding it. Drivers of horse carts, as well as the new private taxis, confronted the choice of going one way or the other around the stone pile. This small pathetic monument forced every driver to pause a moment and consider the changing order.

This morning's edition of *Shkodra* (previously known as *The New Life*) commemorated the birthday of democracy's first martyr, twenty-four-year-old Arben Broci. Along with three others, Broci had been shot dead outside the Party Headquarters in April.

Directly opposite Broci's pile of stones are the remains of the headquarters, its entrance blackened and charred. Inside, the scale of destruction is breathtaking. After the shootings the crowd turned on the building.

The floor tiles had been ripped up, likewise the foundations, even the plumbing.

The wall cladding had been clawed off, picked clean, the windows smashed. On each floor itinerants had left behind piles of human shit and graffiti: Enver mounting his wife, Nexhmije. Or Nexhmije, legs apart, playing with herself alongside an angel with a harp.

It is National Independence Day and back in the Rozala the lobby fills up with old soldiers and cigarette smoke, the sense of special occasion bolstered by the smells of hair oil and shoe polish. Someone hands me a flier drawing attention to a public meeting to be hosted this evening by an American representative of King Leka.

Later in the morning I follow after the old soldiers pouring out of the Rozala with their fedoras, their stylish cigarette holders, their frayed suits.

A substantial crowd has already gathered between the "Heroes of Vigut" and a theatre balcony, where the microphones are being set up.

On the edge of the crowd a young man, turning over sausage meat on a hot coal range, wraps my kebab in a page torn from the works of Enver Hoxha. The page in which my kebab comes wrapped is headed "Failed Strategies" and it reads: "We knew he was bound to come to a bad end . . . Several times we appealed to him to join the National Liberation Movement, but he didn't want to, and . . . he was shot like a stray dog."

Some of the "stray dogs" from the Hoxha era are gathered on the balcony.

First up is Victor Martini, leader of the political prisoners from the Shkodër area. He spent fifteen years in prison. His proposal to rededicate the "Heroes of Vigut" memorial to those thousands killed by the Communists draws the biggest roar of approval.

Pjeter Arbori, after thirty years in prison and recently emerged as the leader of the Democrats in Shkodër, reminds the crowd of the dangers of returning the Socialists to power. This morning's *Shkodra* had ridiculed the Socialists' first conference of five days earlier with the headline:

HOXHA ELECTED FIRST SECRETARY OF SOCIALISTS PARTY. Six years had elapsed since the Great Leader's death, but disciples were still thick on the ground, and many suspected the Socialists' leader, Ramiz Alia, of being a puppet in Nexhmije's control.

When Arbori reminds the crowd of the Socialists' true allegiances, the crowd begins to chant, "Hitler/Hoxha, Hitler/Hoxha . . ."

A poet takes the microphone. His voice is soft and uncertain. He addresses the microphone rather than the crowd: "We are about to remove the bandages. But what is it that we will find? New skin or a scab?" The crowd takes a moment to digest this. There is some shuffling. In the brief silence the poet apparently suffers a crisis of confidence, because next thing he tears the microphone off the stand and, like a demagogue, begins to shout, "Democracy! Democracy!"

Now he has the crowd with him.

But it is time to find Nick's parents' house. Nick had written down his address, but in the hotel all I get from the staff are varying expressions of hopelessness. "Tetori" is a mystery. I ask for a street map, but no such thing exists. One of the waiters stares at the address an inordinate length of time until he is satisfied that he has never heard of it. Another takes me by the wrist and leads me outside. We walk over to the "Heroes of Vigut," where he shades his eyes from the sun and points vaguely in the direction of Greece.

I stop a car travelling barely faster than idling speed. A cigarette butt dangles from the driver's lips. I regret it as soon as I hand over the notebook with Nick's address. The driver has a wild-eyed look about him. "Tetori." He nods. His eyes do a sideways shift to the passenger door.

Shkodër is a maze of tight streets and narrow lanes, some with names, some without. We enter spaces never intended for cars, lanes with high walls of rounded stones, full of promise because of their confined possibilities. But these tight spaces invariably deliver us to a wide boulevard or avenue, and the search begins all over again. Shkodër grows larger by the minute.

Finally I have to beg the man to let me out. Finding Nick's address has become a matter of pride for him.

I wave him to the side of the road. It has come to this. The driver shrugs and pouts. He is sorry, but he is sorry about my lack of faith, too.

I start asking directions all over again. This time a short, dapperly dressed man in a suit and tie threads his arm through mine. He apologises for his lack of English and wonders whether I can speak French, Italian, German, or Russian.

I make a rash claim to "having some French."

"*Ah bien!*" He is delighted. He is a Professor of Languages. Simon Pepa.

Yes, but the Markus' address? I push my dog-eared notebook under his nose—and he nods happily.

His thumb and forefinger pinch the air. We are very close.

"*Près. Près.*"

We walk for another ten minutes. It is a pleasant neighbourhood. We are back among the lanes. The last gold of the grapevines hangs on to rusted trellises. Small cottages of alabaster and stone sit like blushing brides behind walls and fences at eye level.

At some point the Professor tips me at his elbow and we enter a small cottage. I ready myself to embrace the Markus, only to find myself being introduced to the Professor's wife.

I am his first foreigner, he proudly announces.

It is already two in the afternoon. At best I have another two hours to find the Markus. After dark it'll be a hopeless task.

The Professor's twenty-year-old daughter presents a glimmer of hope. She is a beautiful, honey-skinned girl with big brown eyes. In a strange barking voice she explains in English that she attended middle school with Nick's younger brother, Arben. I had confused her the first time when I referred to Nick instead of Ardian.

"So you know the Markus?"

"Very well. Ardian's grandmother lives two doors down." She says Nick used to spend his summers there.

The Professor smiles triumphantly and I begin to relax.

At Nick's grandmother's house, a woman in her mid-thirties comes to the door. As soon as she sees me, she wraps me in a warm hug. Nick has sent word ahead.

She sends her two daughters, Alma and Nicoletta, to escort me to the Markus' house. The address is in the very neighbourhood I had cruised through with the wild-eyed driver earlier in the afternoon. At the time I couldn't understand why he kept asking after the "Markus" instead of the name of the rruga. We arrive back here on dark.

The truck driver's house is larger than the Professor's house. There is no resemblance at all between Nick, the aesthete, and his father, a ponderous grey man in his fifties. The father quietly retreats behind his wife's excited welcome. Nick's brother speaks a little English.

I spill out the contents of my bag, but there is no rush to inspect the radio or the books. Nick's father takes the cigarettes and walks out of the room with them.

Mrs. Marku brings in a tray of coffee. Since I am invited to dinner, Nick's father, who is putting on his coat and hat, has decided that it will be a tediously long evening if we can't understand each other. Nick's brother, Arben, explains that his father will fetch his niece Mimi, a schoolteacher, who lives five kilometres away. Through the window, in the lengthening shadows I glimpse Mr. Marku setting off on his bicycle.

Meanwhile, I get to see the bedroom which Arben now has to himself. Dragging out a carton from under his brother's bed, Arben says he was surprised to find how much Nick had hidden from him.

There are a few treasured pages of The Financial Times and The Independent cadged from the tourists Nick had fished for with his quick piercing glances in the gardens across from the Rozala. On two occasions he had brought tourists to the house, something his father discouraged, since the risk was considerable, and there had been arguments, and promises from Nick that he wouldn't do it again.

In the carton were Nick's notebooks. One was entitled "English from TV." Another contained German phrases. With these snatches of language he had lured foreigners to the "blind spot" behind Lenin's statue.

Nick quickly befriended them with his intelligence. Foreigners would one day be his way out. He had amassed a huge correspondence. Letters to the Red Cross in half a dozen European countries. Letters from his "family" in Holland, Germany, and England. Pinned to his bedroom wall was a large map of the North Yorkshire moors, with a dotted line to indicate the trail hiked by his English friends.

It was extraordinary what he had collected. The words to pop songs. Western icons faithfully listed—Michael Jackson, Samantha Fox, Phil Collins, Duran Duran, Joe Cocker, Elton John. A street map of London and the Underground map. A red pen traced the blue route from Victoria Station to Islington Station. Nick had everything planned ahead. The moment he arrived in Heathrow he would find his own way.

His friends had sent his fare money tucked away in a secret compartment of an envelope. In one letter advising Nick of the arrangements, there was this reassurance: "Don't worry, Phil knows about these kinds of things." I imagined two or three slightly goofy English lads with daytime computer jobs and sea cadet backgrounds, thrilling to Nick's cause.

People had sent him books. Nick had translated "The Final Problem" from the *Celebrated Cases of Sherlock Holmes*. He had pencilled in translations down the column margins of Robert Burns and Walt Whitman.

The notebooks, the treasured sections of English newspapers, the letters—all in one sense, at least, belonged to a life already abandoned. In Rome, unless he discovered some vices, there would be no need to lead a life as furtive as this one.

———

Before, in the bedroom, Arben had told me about Nick's involvement in last winter's demonstration. Their cousin Kolec had been one of the organisers and Nick had begged to be included. The plan had been to pull down the statue of Stalin. On the day of the demonstration two thousand brave souls gathered in the piazza. Police with guns took up positions on the rooftop of the Rozala. But, incredibly, they shot only film. They filmed everything, and the next day they began their arrests.

Nick hid all his books, his English newspapers, and waited for the police to call. Ten of his friends, Kolec included, were rounded up.

Kolec was interrogated repeatedly. The film taken by the police had caught Nick's shoulder and the police insisted to Kolec that he could identify the shoulder in the film.

Kolec held out; finally the police gave up and sent him to Qale-Barit to work as a miner. No sooner had Kolec arrived than he organised a hunger strike. The prison was closed down and the prisoners sent elsewhere, Kolec to Burrell.

Then in July he was given an early release and granted a visa to travel to Italy.

Arben has a photograph of Nick and Kolec at a restaurant in Padua. Their glasses are raised. A bottle of wine has been drunk. Nick is in a T-shirt, his face radiant with summer health. A freer spirit is evident here than the pale student patrolling the cold monastery floors in Rome.

Before Mimi arrived, Arben had asked me not to mention the demonstration, Kolec, or Nick's involvement. Mimi's husband is *sigourimi*. A very dangerous man, said Arben.

Mimi turned out to be completely unguarded. She laughed a lot. Her eyes brimmed trustingly beneath purple eyeliner . . . I thought of her sitting on Mr. Marku's handlebars—pedalled across Shkodër to interpret for a foreigner. I thought of Mr. Marku patiently waiting with his bike while his niece scrambled to put on makeup and a favourite, knee-length black dress.

"You like it?" She was pleased. "Vlady bought it for me. He buys all my clothes," she said.

"Really?" I said. Then I asked how she had met her husband, while pretending not to notice the nervous glance exchanged between Arben and his father.

But Mimi was unconcerned by my curiosity. She said they had met on a bus. Vladimir was attending the special Ministry of Internal Affairs school in Tirana. Mimi was studying political philosophy in Tirana. They had met on the bus returning to Shkodër.

She said matter-of-factly, "I cannot tell you anything about his work, because he does not tell me anything."

It was later, after we had put away the last few bottles of Nick's father's wine, the product off his back-yard vine, that Mimi herself started to wonder how she had come to marry into the sigourimi.

She shook her head. "We met on the bus." She shrugged. Then she laughed. Nick's mother, happy that Mimi was making the evening such a success, kissed her niece on the cheek.

"I met my husband on the bus. He asked to see my biografi. After that, we got married. Perhaps it happens differently in the West?"

It all seemed to have been so simple. Now, she said, she

no longer felt the same. "I have never loved him. We live as if by arrangement."

The Markus, none the wiser for Mimi's sad confession, raised their glasses for a toast. Mimi smiled and met each of their glasses with her own.

Mimi said she had grown up with a portrait of the Great Leader in her family's living room. It was hung on the wall opposite the window, where people passing by could see Enver prominently displayed.

"My father," she said, "recently took down the portrait, because in Albania, as you know, we have run out of glass."

13

In the morning, as Mimi had promised to arrange, Nick's old schoolteacher Gjyzepina Lulgjuzay is waiting down in the lobby. She appears matronly, in a man's jacket, a thick plaid skirt, and flat shoes.

We are both a little wary of each other at first.

Gjyzepina begins by running through the morning newspapers. In one paper a cartoon has Albania separated from its borders with Greece, Macedonia, and Montenegro, merrily sailing for Europe while a chain anchored to a sickle stretches to breaking point.

Gjyzepina laughs—revealing just two yellowing teeth in her mouth. She suddenly remembers this, and up comes her hand and an unguarded moment sadly trails off to embarrassment.

We wander off to the piazza. Gjyzepina talks about Nick. Of course she remembers him. Nick was one of her best students.

It is National Liberation Day, but unlike yesterday's National Independence Day, there is hardly a soul about.

Cliff had sketched a quick map of the piazza and its surrounding attractions for me. The Atheists Museum should be the two-storey building opposite. But according to Gjyzepina, the museum has been abandoned. The icons have been returned to the churches. For a brief time the Atheists Museum was home to the Democrats, but the protests following the Socialists' unexpected election victory earlier in the year had blocked the piazza and the Democrats were moved to a former church kindergarten.

"It is not far from here," she says.

Rruga Ndre Mjeda is a narrow, winding lane which begins behind a café. We catch up with people trailing through the doors of San Antonio.

Until a year ago the church had been a gymnasium. The concrete bleachers are still in place at the rear of the church. Voices whisper in darkness. In the foyer there is just enough light to make out photographs of priests and bishops tortured and executed by the regime.

Cliff had told me to look in the Atheists Museum for the photographs of priests armed with machine guns firing into groups of partisans.

The priest's house alongside the Church of San Antonio is a pile of rubble. Sparrows hop nervously between lumps of plaster and concrete, an area of waste stretching up to the doorway of the old kindergarten, now the Democrats' office.

Rruga Ndre Mjeda comes out at the old Cathedral of

Shkodër. We arrive in time to see a donkey carrying rubble out of the cathedral doors. With the help of Italian money, the cathedral is in the process of reverting from a volleyball court. There, above the altar, the time clock is still attached. Back outside the cathedral a mob of teenage girls surrounds an Italian priest. He's wearing designer sunglasses and his tanned cheeks bulge with pleasure at all this attention.

Two old Albanian priests stand off at a short distance, basking in the sunshine. We learn that both had been jailed—one for ten years. But neither will talk about his experiences.

"God forgives," the older one says. "We must look to the future."

Another fifteen minutes' amble and we come onto kisha e Volreve Katolike, the Catholic cemetery, in the Skanderbeg district, a poor, run-down area on the edge of town. Newly painted white crosses hide under the shade of trees. Work in the chapel had started the previous November, two months before the first demonstrations against the regime.

Gjyzepina hadn't believed at first what she heard about people bringing the church bell out of hiding and turning up with paint and brushes.

"We were afraid to see who was building the church. Even me! To tell the truth, I put a handkerchief over my head and came here in the night with my brother to see for myself.

"After all these years," she says. "I think the rebuilding of the church was the people's way of telling the Party that we could do anything without first asking them."

Alongside the photographs of the slain priests in the

Church of San Antonio had been others of Shkodër's first public Mass, coming nearly twenty-five years after the regime declared the country to be the world's first atheist state.

Before a terrified congregation the priest that day—the previous November—observed, "I see it written in your eyes. You are ready to die."

We wander about the graves under the trees. Some carry photographs of the dead. Where a portrait hasn't been available, a drawn arrow indicates the deceased, a smiling face at the back of a family gathering; with those who had been older, or gravely ill, it sometimes seemed that they were already posing for their headstones. The other graves, the ones without headstones and for a long time lost in overgrown grass, have re-emerged, their grave markings defined by carefully placed whitewashed pebbles.

Another country was emerging through grainy, poorly reproduced photographs appearing daily in newspapers, testifying to some wrongdoing, or defending after forty years some slander by the Party on someone's parent, grandparent, sister, brother, aunt or uncle. Family pride, as much as it had always done in Albania, was seeking to put right old wrongs.

Right up until King Zog's era, defending family honour offered grounds for taking another's life. Shkodër had been notorious for its blood feuds. An imagined slight, "high words" at a card game, was often enough for a man to shoot his neighbour dead. Vengeance was routinely expected and a man might stand vigil near his neighbour's house for days, a rifle laid across his knee, in order to exact the blood "owed" him.

Joseph Swire tells of sharing a room at the old Hotel International with Avni Rustem, the man who assassinated Zog's Turkophile uncle, Essad Pasha, in Paris in 1920. The French convicted Rustem of political murder and fined him one franc. Rustem returned to Albania, where his countrymen rewarded him with a pension. Swire described a "little pale-faced man in threadbare tweeds . . ." He liked him. Rustem cheerfully told Swire over his newspaper that he was waiting for his death, for Essad's blood had to be avenged. Six weeks later he was shot down in Tirana by a hireling of Essad's family, "a thick man with a red face" whom Swire says he had met several times in 1930 near his house "with an innocent umbrella in his hand."

The priests and the teenage girls were gone when we wandered back past the cathedral. Not a soul was about, even at the residential end of Rruga Ndre Mjeda. Shkodër's population turns indoors between the hours of one and three.

A mangy cat lying in a doorway raised its head as we passed. A single vendor had chosen to stay with his five or six copies of Albert Camus's *The Stranger*, which was enjoying the runaway success of a newly released hot title.

It was at the bottom end of the rruga that we came upon a small crowd lined up outside an open door.

The building seemed to be some kind of shrine. A new enterprise, something like Bill would imagine, a highly popular café even crossed my mind.

"It is not these things," says Gjyzepina. "It is . . . How do you say . . . ?"

She thought for the moment, concentrating with the effort. "It is the house of biografi."

"A house?"

"No. Not a house exactly. An office."

We chewed around some more, before nailing it down to the office for political prisoners.

I preferred Gjyzepina's original choice.

"House of biografi did you say?"

"Yes," she says. "This is the place."

14

In a back room of the house of biografi there is a desk and two chairs. The registrar sits before a huge open ledger, into which he enters the details of the person sitting opposite.

The room is filled with surviving relatives. Adult children with stories of parents carried off in the night. Wives who have lost touch with their husbands. Or solitary men and women, former prisoners and exiles whose lives were confiscated under the old regime, have been lining up in Rruga Ndre Mjeda to tell their story.

Two lines form in this small cool room of alabaster. One behind the registrar's desk, and another line before me and Gjyzepina.

It just happened this way, a story for the ledger and another for me. They present their lives as though they are little more than damaged houseware, bits of crockery; as if to say, Here, do with it what you may.

In Albania when lives disappeared it was more often than not through a trapdoor called "Article 55," shorthand for "agitation, betrayal, and propaganda." The first time I ask a man who had been jailed for ten years for the evidence, some details please of his "betraying the people," he doesn't quite understand.

"The evidence? The evidence is they said I betrayed the people."

Then he says, "When they said 'Ten years,' it felt to me that they had kissed me on both cheeks."

One woman refuses to come farther than the doorway. She is halfway through giving her details when she loses her nerve. The registrar assures her that she is amongst friends. She mustn't feel afraid.

"It is not for myself that I feel afraid," she says. "I am afraid for my children."

The *sigourimi* recently dynamited some houses in her street. She does not want her house to be next. She says she is sorry; she cannot go through with her story. It is still much too dangerous.

Luchia Cole steps forward. She had worked in a bakery. In the late seventies, during one of the country's periodic convulsions, the biografis were pored over for likely victims and it was discovered that Luchia's father had escaped the country in 1951. After eleven months of interrogation, Luchia "confessed" to her crime and was jailed eight years under Article 55.

Gjenovefa Vilaku is here on her husband's behalf. Before their marriage, before they had even met, her husband was studying in Yugoslavia, where he fell in love with a Hungarian student. After his return home his letters were intercepted and he was accused of collaborating with a foreign agent. A death sentence was commuted to seven years.

The day of his arrest, his uncle, a priest, was executed.

He was jailed a second time for "agitation and propaganda" after the sigourimi found a "second witness" who was a spy in prison.

"Where is your husband now?"

"Germany."

When word of the rush on Embassy Row trickled up to Shkodër, the entire family packed up, ready. At the last moment, Gjenovefa's mother fell sick and she elected to stay behind. The next she heard from her husband was a postcard from Hamburg.

Bepin Dacaj's father, at the age of sixty, was jailed for thirteen years after discussing democracy with "friends" in the piazza of Shkodër. Sent to Ballsh Zejmen, the professor of English had his teeth broken and forks stuck up behind his fingernails.

"They tortured my father until he confessed. He had a heart ailment and couldn't endure it."

The professor's wife then divorced him to preserve the "correctness" of her biografi. Nevertheless, she and Bepin were forced into an exile's life in Elbasan, where for fifteen years he worked as a farm labourer.

Six months ago, Bepin had walked away from the camp. He set out for his father's prison. But when he got there they could show him only his old cell. They didn't know where they had buried him.

For hour after hour I felt confronted by a "blood feud" tradition perversely altered to where now the Party had adopted for itself the position of an aggrieved victim that was "owed blood." The registrar said between four and five thousand people with "bad biografi" were penalised or jailed every year. He invited me to multiply that number by forty-five years.

The place-names I hear of in Rruga Ndre Mjeda can be found on any map: Spaq Mirdita, Kavajë, Elbasan, Fier, Lushnje. Each is accompanied by a black dot or a circle to indicate population size, a town or a village; a grape or pneumatic drill similarly identifies horticulture or mining.

In that sense they are owned up to. They are places of sunshine and the grape on postcards, but have a second identity as places of exile and misery.

I doubt whether Cliff could have visited the latter. In fact, I'm sure he didn't. The photographs of Cliff in Albania show him laughing among friends at the beach in Durrës and Sarandë. On the map that Cliff gave me these places are identified by sun umbrellas.

The house of biografi closes between one and three o'clock each day.

"Business hours," says the registrar, without any humour intended.

We wander out to the lane. The sheer weight of these histories is numbing. This morning a man, Zef Marana, broke down after describing how he had concealed the death of a cellmate in Burrell prison for five days so he could get the dead man's food. He had been sentenced to fifteen years in jail after trying to swim across the Lake of Shkodër to Yugoslavia. He had got within three hundred metres of the Yugoslav shore when a boat drew alongside. Glancing up, he had seen soldiers with their rifles drawn.

We are recovering in the sunshine in the rubble of the

priest's former house, when a woman in a plastic raincoat stops to speak with Gjyzepina, and it begins all over again.

"This woman here," starts Gjyzepina; she has been given to understand that I am "collecting lives."

Pina Dushaj had worked in a liquor store near a hydro-electric plant. This had been around the time of Enver's split from the "Chinese deviationists." As many of the liquor store customers had been Chinese technicians, Pina was accused of "betraying the people" and sentenced to thirteen years' imprisonment in Kocova. In an act of self-preservation, her husband had divorced her. Her two children had been sent to an orphanage.

The woman is finished telling her story now, and there is an awkward moment, a feeling of an uneven transaction having run its course. It had been easier in the office, where another person was always on hand, ready to take someone else's place. A momentum kept things going, and appalling as it seems, sometimes there was hardly time to thank the person—in the absence of anything else suitable to say— before the next in line was bending down to correct the spelling of her name in my notebook.

The woman continues to stand there, staring at this collector of lives.

I ask her age. I can't think what else to say.

I write down fifty-seven, until Gjyzepina corrects me.

"I said thirty-seven."

"Are you sure?"

"Yes, I am sure."

"What about the leather bits in her bag?"

"She works at home as a seamstress for an Italian business."

And on it goes, to the point of banality. I ask after the bitten end of a stick of bread in her bag.

Gjyzepina says Pina had waited in line for three hours for the bread.

"It was either the bread or line up before the registrar in Rruga Mjeda. She could not decide."

Gjyzepina offers some gentle words and the woman nods that she understands the interview is over. We continue to sit on the rocks in the sun and watch the woman drag herself up the lane to the cathedral.

"I also have a story to tell," says Gjyzepina.

It concerns the engineer brother of her husband, Clement. The brother had worked on a hydroelectric plant.

His supervisor had wanted to send him to France to study, so Clement's brother set about learning French. He studied until late at night. Any time off work was given over to study. He was going to France. His friends knew this; his family. Everyone was proud. The departure time approached and rolled past. He was told he could not leave the country because of some difficulty with his biografi.

"Clement's father was very distressed. He went to the Party. He said, 'Please, I beg you, tell me what I can do to improve my biografi.' "

"And?"

"Nothing. Clement's brother had learnt a language for which he had no use. This failing, too, was added to his biografi."

15

The Markus are waiting for me back in the Rozala. The glimpse through the doors is a forbidding one of the father, solemn and uncommunicative in his buttoned-up coat. The son is craning his neck to look for other company, another world to explore.

Since it is dark, the Markus have forbidden me to walk alone. At night I must be accompanied, and on this point Nick's father is surprisingly forthright.

There are gunshots all night, and every night, he says.

I had been woken by gunshots as early on as my first night in Tirana. Bill seemed to think it had to do with wedding ceremonies. "The guys get loaded and start trying to shoot the stars out of the sky." Some kind of tradition, he thought.

I pass this on to a puzzled Arben.

I have not heard of this thing, he says.

However, it is the father's comment that bandits are responsible for the gunfire which draws a derisive reaction from the son.

"It is the fault of the police. Everybody knows they do it deliberately to intimidate the people, to stop them from gathering."

There was a surprise waiting at the Markus' house. While still out in the street we could hear the music. Inside, the music blared from the new tape deck. Sprawled along the couch with his ear glued to the speaker was Mimi's husband, Vladimir, a man in his thirties with a well-fed face. Chopped sideburns. Black trousers pulled tight over heavy thighs.

Mimi intercepted me inside the door with a nervous handshake. Last night we had parted with the customary kiss.

She started to say something, then gave up and went to plead with her husband to turn down the music.

Arben hauled me into his bedroom. "Please. Not a word about Vladimir's work. Don't ask him anything."

We filed into the living room, the scene of last night's drinking and fun, some of it at Vladimir's expense. Mimi said the Party had thought Vladimir too dangerous to be a card-carrying member.

I suspect he might draw pleasure from such a reputation. The very idea of it seemed to be tucked inside his cheek.

It was terribly awkward to begin with. Mimi's husband drumrolled his fingers along the top of the couch. He spread his legs and planted his feet wide. He had the couch to himself and we were his audience.

He tapped a little tune out on the couch; then he looked up and spoke quickly to Mimi.

She said, "Vlady wishes you to ask him anything you wish. Anything at all."

"Anything?" I checked with Mimi. I wondered what she had returned home with last night. "He is aware that I know he is *sigourimi*?"

There was some mocking laughter from Vladimir when he heard the word.

"Ask me," he said, apishly thumping his chest.

I described to Vladimir the faces I had seen in the little

room off Rruga Ndre Mjeda. I passed on some of the stories I had heard of lives destroyed by lies and deceits. The "friend's" evidence. The jacked-up "second witness." The creation of a martyred caste.

I mentioned the example of Kolec Jak Simoni, whose story was still fresh in my memory. He had been jailed ten years under Article 55 after speaking among "friends" of escape. He had no idea who these supposed friends were. The conversation had never taken place. Then in 1978 he received another ten-year sentence after the biografis were opened and it was discovered that Kolec had two relatives who had escaped the country back in the fifties.

Mimi, of course, had to pass all this on. Her husband listened with interest. He perched on the edge of the couch, elbows on knees, staring off into the distance.

It was too much to try to defend, and to his credit he didn't even try to. Instead, for the next hour or so he explained the role of the sigourimi in all of this. He counted off on his fingers the points he wished to make.

First, any information is valuable. It is not important who the informant is—only the information. Nor was there any verification of the information.

"For example, I betray you to the sigourimi. The matter is taken up between you and them. I am forgotten."

This point, he said, had been unique to Albania.

Second, under the guidance of the Great Leader, the revolution had to express everything. Nothing could be concealed.

Thirdly, he said, promotion within the sigourimi depended on gathering information and informants. Promotion was not supported by financial gain, but a moral or political purity was created. "The Party asked the *sigourimi* to find enemies. When they could not find real enemies they had to invent them."

"You understand what Vlady is saying," said Mimi. "Had we continued to go on this way, the country would have consumed itself."

Vladimir said the system had been like an alter ego. He could not tell Mimi these things because she, in turn, might tell her relatives.

By now I had the feeling he was doing more than simply explaining a concept to a stranger. There was a sense of sharing an intimate confidence; shortly afterwards he excused himself to go outside to smoke a cigarette.

"I have never heard him mention these things before. This is the first time ever," Arben whispered excitedly.

It was extraordinary that a simple task such as explaining an institutional concept could take on such a personal dimension.

Nick's father didn't want it to proceed any further. This kind of talk distressed him. While Vladimir was out of the room he told Mimi he wanted the conversation to shift to something more pleasant. I had the feeling he was operating in the old climate of fear, where it was better to know nothing because information invariably meant complicity. You learnt something and immediately were tainted by it. Either you became a threat because of what you knew or you were made a victim because of it.

Mrs. Marku was ready to serve dinner. Another bottle of wine was dusted off. To appease Nick's father we discussed books.

I brought up Kadare for discussion, Dossier H, but its mention produced only a scowl. Kadare, in Vladimir's view, had disgraced himself by leaving the country. This was not an uncommon view. Even Gjyzepina was critical.

Yesterday, while walking up Rruga Ndre Mjeda, I had asked for her opinion of Kadare. She said, "How can we say he wrote honestly? Perhaps he fought for democracy with his heart and mind, but he forgot to express it."

Vladimir put down his fork and with his fingers pulled a chewed hunk of meat from his mouth. Then he held up a greasy finger to make his point. Kadare, he said, was a propagandist.

"Yes," said Mimi. "My husband is referring to The Great Winter, the novel in which Enver Hoxha is the main character. The hero."

Vladimir patted Mimi's shoulder. She had on the same black dress as last night. Mimi looked at where he had left a grease spot; Vladimir dove back into his food.

I wondered who Vladimir thought was behind the gunfire at night.

"Bandits," he said, with his mouth full, and went on eating. This time Arben did not contest it.

After Mimi and Vladimir left, Nick's mother wrapped a cake in a towel and placed it in my hands.

"My mother would like you to take the cake to Nick in Rome," Arben explained.

It was a special cake which the Catholics in the north of the country baked to celebrate Easter. In the past, Arben explained, they had had to bake the cake secretly, even going to the extent of burying the eggshells in the back yard so the neighbours wouldn't see them in the rubbish and tell the *sigourimi*.

"Vladimir?" I asked.

Arben nodded.

"Vladimir," his mother said.

16

The next morning the entire delegation is there to see me off—Gjyzepina, Clement, Arben, Nick's parents.

True to her word, Gjyzepina has gone off to search the neighbourhood for someone to accompany me to Tirana. She turns up with Marcello, a greying twenty-nine-year-old student returning to university in Tirana.

The bus, in fact, is an old lorry which draws up to the meat market at great speed, splashing ditch water over the bloody carcasses displayed on the pavement.

Fifteen or twenty passengers are already standing on the tray, and because I am the inexperienced foreigner and because I am surrounded by fifteen to twenty willing hosts, I'm pushed with Marcello to the front of the tray to lean up against the cab. Marcello tells me this is the most sought-after place—here it is warm and secure.

Within a short time, out in the countryside, my head is a block of ice. And what was exhilarating has lost its edge. Behind us the other passengers' eyelids are half-closed, their faces red with cold, their hair swept back off their foreheads by the breeze. They stand with their legs apart and their hands placed on the shoulders of the person in front of them.

Arben said we would be in Tirana in a couple of hours, no more.

Now Marcello tells me it's likely to be "three, four hours, perhaps."

Every so often there is a respite as we slow up behind a horse and cart. Briefly, the icy breeze subsides and we thaw out in the still air. It is possible again to feel the sun and imagine the greenness either side of the road in flower or baked in midsummer. The season of postcards. Then we're off again, lurching, the tray leaping potholes with its human cargo. The words of Marcello's uncertain English suddenly pop up shrilly or are blown away into the jet stream, and it is some time before I understand that he is trying to tell me about the *sigourimi*.

"You are interested in such things. Gjyzepina told me."

We slow down for another cart piled high with hay, and in the brief stillness his words and sentences are delivered in a comprehensible form.

Some years ago, he says, an officer from the Ministry of Internal Affairs had approached him with a request for information. The question of refusal had to be balanced against consideration of his family's prospects, and Marcello had tried to hedge.

Each day the same man had come to him with the same request. "Please, Marcello, what can you tell me? About anything, anyone. Tell me about your neighbour."

Each day Marcello shrugged and said, "We'll see." Time passes, and he begins to wonder if he has won this battle.

The *sigourimi* stops visiting. The pestering ends. But shortly after this, Marcello learns that he is being tailed, that his conversations are being noted.

The lorry has started to move off again and Marcello is a torrent of words. The hay bales pass at eye level as the truck overtakes the cart. The breeze picks up, the passengers press together, words fly through the air.

This is the last bit that I catch: the final revelation. His neighbour had placed a listening device in the ceiling of his family's living room.

"My neighbour!" he says.

The wind grew stronger and we herded closer together. Marcello stood tall with his shirt collar open to the bruising cold, and I crept away to thoughts of Cliff.

I had looked him up with the sincerest of motives. I had wanted information of the most obvious kind—where to go, some useful phrases: "Milk, no sugar, please." What to eat, what not to eat, whom to meet, whom to avoid. And as expected, Cliff had graciously come through for me.

There were the surprises that come with establishing contact with anyone after a number of years. I mean Cliff's behaviour, which, when all was said and done, I had thought no more than mildly eccentric. For example, his forceful invitation to exchange my shoes for his range of rubber jandals at the door. The jandals and the living conditions in the basement were curiosities, peculiar to Cliff. There had been no means, or even the thought, of tracing them to another place.

The ritualised hospitality, the boiling of water over Bunsen burners, the insistent invitations to eat more, more, and more. The same worrying over details, the placement of cups and the order in which the coffee followed the raki, the cake coming after the sour pickles, the piles of rubber jandals behind every doorway—all the things I had thought peculiar to Cliff had popped up at Simon Pepa's house, then again at the Markus' and Gjyzepina's.

And then there was Cliff's appearance. His period look. The wild mane of hair and the sideburns he'd grown to reconstruct himself in the image of Balkan Man. But none of this had seemed particularly obvious to me at the time. Bess had more than hinted: "How Cliff has changed." But nothing had quite the impact of those first glimpses at Durrës, those bedraggled locks of hair, the triangular sideburns, the frayed bell-bottoms. Until then I had had no idea of the extent to which Cliff had entered into the spirit of his adopted homeland. But certainly after Durrës, and perhaps even before then, I had sneakily known that I wouldn't be able to leave Cliff out of this.

Cliff had been helpful with contacts, one of them Illir Ikonomi, whom Cliff had described as responsible for writing replies to Radio Tirana's worldwide correspondents.

I found Radio Tirana a short distance from the Hoxha Memorial, in a residential street. Building had commenced on the new Italian embassy opposite, where a plainclothesman with an AK-47 patrolled that side of the street.

For an acquaintance of Cliff's, Illir was not at all what I had been expecting. A short, squat man with frizzy hair, he met me in the lobby of Radio Tirana, wearing a denim jacket and jeans, in stark contrast to the darkly uniformed security guards who rigorously controlled the flow in and out of the building.

Of even greater surprise was his faint American accent. And a little later, in what suggested a remarkable transformation for a former broadcaster of propaganda, he mentioned in passing that he was now a stringer for Reuters.

We climbed the stairs to the foreign service floor. Radio Tirana broadcasts in twenty-two languages—among them Persian, broadcasts of which had started around the time of the Iranian revolution, Illir said. In those days Tirana had been hopeful that the Iranian revolutionaries would choose the correct path. The broadcasts had been designed to guide them on this matter.

Cliff had shown me photographs of Radio Tirana's transmitter towers outside Durrës. I remembered the way he put on his glasses and held up the towers as examples of brilliant Albanian engineering. But Illir now told me that the towers had been built by the Chinese.

Illir had started with Radio Tirana's first broadcasts to China in 1978.

"This was at a time when relations with China had deteriorated. There were ideological issues at stake," he said. "The duty of the China service was to try and convince the Chinese people that their path was the wrong one."

However, the service failed to receive a single letter from China. Not even a postcard. There were some very sound reasons for this. One, he said, was that the broadcast was barely strong enough to be heard in China. Two, shortwave-radio sets were rare items in China.

Illir seemed to find this amusing, too. The idea of

providing a broadcast which had no hope of reaching its targeted audience had kept him fully employed for years.

Response to the station's other broadcasts was considerably better. Radio Tirana received seven thousand letters annually.

"Well, that's not bad, is it?"

"Radio Vaticana receives annually one hundred and twenty thousand letters," he said.

We wandered along the foreign service floor to the news room. Ancient Imperial typewriters sat on desks in a small cramped space. On the walls were old maps—on one it was still possible to find Rhodesia.

I happened to look out the window and caught sight of a man with a rifle slung over his shoulder, walking over the rooftops.

Illir shrugged.

"Security," he offered. Otherwise he had no idea what the man was doing, stalking the rooftops.

"And this here is my desk." Then he turned and introduced me to the young man sitting opposite, at the "Turkish desk."

In the studio, they were mixing the previous day's "Beatles concert" performed by Albanian musicians.

"Why the Beatles?" I wondered.

"Why of course, to show the Beatles have arrived in Albania." He managed to grin.

17

Around the time of the Beatles hits "Love Me Do," "She Loves You," and "I Want to Hold Your Hand," Harry Hamm, the first German reporter allowed to visit Albania since the war, had come away with descriptions of "golden busts of Enver between the palm fronds or the eucalyptus leaves . . . Enver's picture was hung alongside the sleazy beer tent on the beach, as a pennant at the edge of a football field, or decorating an archaeological collection in a provincial museum—even walls of cowsheds on collective farms." Hamm was continually surprised by organised groups ready to chant Enver's name whenever the slightest opportunity arose.

Even now, six years after the Emperor's death, it was still possible to find traces of the person Shapallo had had to measure up to.

The morning after I arrived back from Shkodër I wandered across to the Enver Hoxha Memorial. It was extremely cold, and paper-thin ice cracked under the wheels of the few early-morning cyclists.

Although it had been given a new name, the new National Cultural Centre did nothing to conceal features which so manifestly honour a pharaoh. The huge pyramid-shaped edifice of glass and marble had been designed by Enver's architect son-in-law, Klement Kolaneci. You enter at basement level and climb two flights of stairs to the main display area. Up until a few months earlier visitors had caught their breath here and gazed across the marble floor to a twenty-five-tonne sculpture of Enver.

The Emperor, in "deified form," is still there to be seen in old postcards on sale downstairs. In these, a strip of red carpet marches across the marble floor to the feet of the seated Emperor. In the postcard sculpture, I noticed, Enver's genial features had been given a firmer line; a feeling of intractability is further conveyed by the sculptor's placement of a hand on each knee.

Since the Emperor was removed, the light that showers down from a copper ceiling, shaped into a star to reflect the world's five continents, these days falls onto a faded block.

On the upper floors most of the display items had been removed—but not all. Enver's Fiat Millicento, the one reputedly used by him during the war, was still there, a brilliant emerald finish with a black trim, as shiny as new, on flat tyres.

Around one corner the man himself gave me a terrible fright. A mere life-size sculpture of Enver standing, like a figure from a crowd, with his hands in his pockets.

Bits of sticking plaster covered the walls. Nearly all the photographs had been taken down and stored.

On the next floor, I did find a few photographs still up. One spectacular photo of a May Day procession showed thousands of Tirana schoolchildren moulded into the letters of PARTI ENVER marching down Stalingrad Boulevard.

The real surprise, however, was the library. It had been pretty much left alone. Obviously it had been designed to be viewed at a distance, a library as vista, rather than one in which books were meant to be picked up and handled, because every book in the Hoxha collection was not what it appeared to be. The chapters on *Questions of Agrarian Politics in the Soviet Union* bear a cover with the name Herman Melville. Alain Guerin's *Le General Gris* contains upside-down pages filled with sketches of generators. Emile Zola's *Reconte par sa fille* considers political deviation in the Soviet Union. *The Life of Tolstoy* tackles the problems of collectivisation. *Histoire de l'Art* contains Stalin's thoughts on Lenin. Robert Kemp's *Life of the Book* turns out to be a dissertation on "liquidation of the Kulak [the wealthy peasant class] in the Soviet Union."

Also in the library, a faded reproduction had been blown up to such a size that the screened dots were visible. The photograph had zeroed in on a section of Spanish Party of Labour supporters at a rally in Madrid. Presumably the photograph had earned its place as proof of the Emperor's popularity abroad.

The overall desired effect had best been achieved in a video which pilgrims to the memorial were encouraged to buy as a souvenir of their visit. The video begins with a bird's-eye view over the pyramid. Slowly the camera eye descends and we enter the ceiling to choral music, and there he is, the Emperor in a haze of golden light. The choral music fades away and in cathedral silence we are left to gaze, at a respectful distance, at Enver's twenty-five-tonne presence.

Albanians had shown a partiality to kings and queens, and in the twenties emissaries had been sent abroad to shop for likely candidates.

A Colonel Aubrey Herbert, about whom little is known, was nevertheless a candidate for a short while. Another was the British long-jump champion and cricketer C. B. Fry, who during a visit to a Balkan dignitary in Geneva was asked of his interest in the kingship.

The cricketer wasted no time in accepting but fell out of calculation after a disappointing assessment from a visiting Albanian bishop.

Several London newspapers took up the cause, prompting a number of unsolicited applicants. Among these were a naval cadet and a dancing instructress.

A more likely contender was the First Earl of Inchcape, whose lunch at his castle in Ayrshire was interrupted by his butler with news that a visitor from London had arrived to offer the Earl the throne of Albania.

The Earl wiped his mouth with a napkin and asked, "Where is it?"

A letter of formal offer arrived the next day:

> I do not know whether this is the first time in your career that you have been offered a kingdom, and I fully realise of course this is a matter that you could not consider seriously, especially in view of the fact that the new King would be expected to do all in his power financially and politically to help in construction of railways, roads, schools and public buildings throughout the country.
>
> Perhaps next time you are cruising in the Mediterranean you would feel drawn to put in at Valona or Durazzo in order to express your sentiments, whatever they be, in connection with the offer which I am seriously putting before you.
>
> In any case, if you turn it down entirely, perhaps you would feel called upon to suggest the name of

some wealthy Englishman or American with administrative power who would care to take up the cudgels on Albania's behalf, thereby securing the honourable position as Albania's King.

Inchcape's reply was as follows: "It is a great honour to be offered the throne, but I'm afraid it is not in my line."

Last night Marcello turned up at the Dajti to tell me that King Leka's representative was in town. An American professor, Nderim Kupi.

"Nephew of Abas Agha Kupi," he said portentously.

Marcello had heard the King's representative speak at the Tirana University campus that afternoon, as well in Shkodër, when dinner with the Markus had prevented me from attending.

Marcello said everyone had been handed posters of King Leka I—to familiarise themselves with the Albanian King. There in the Dajti lobby he unfurled a poster of a tall, sombre man in a general's uniform.

I checked with the desk, then with Marcello walked briskly across Skanderbeg Square to the Tirana Hotel, and the desk clerk there said, "Yes, we have a Nderim Kupi. He left the hotel half an hour ago."

"To go where?"

"The airport, sir."

18

Kings and queens, as well as witches and goblins, were staging a comeback—this was the news coming out of Shtepia Boteuse Naim Frasheri, the State Publishing House.

Fatos Kongoli had been in the director's chair for less than three months. His office was impressively large, but bare, as though still waiting for Fatos to make his presence felt. It was also very cold. It was late afternoon and Fatos still hadn't shed his overcoat.

His hands never left his pockets as he crossed the office blowing small white clouds of breath ahead of him.

"I am sorry. My English is not very good." He excused himself for a moment and returned with one of his English-speaking editors, Brikena.

I mentioned my interest in biografi—which drew a chuckle from him.

Fatos explained how it was the director's right to see all the files of the publishing house's employees. Before he assumed the position, it had occurred to him at odd times of the day—sometimes at night in bed, or while walking to work in the morning—that finally, in a matter of days, he would be able to take a look at his own file. His curiosity mounted, overwhelmingly so, blotting out all other thoughts. But in the end, drawing pleasure from denial, he had resisted.

"I decided I could not bear to see what my friends had said about me."

In another two months, he said, the files office would be closing forever. After that, the only files on record would be of a résumé nature.

Brikena went out to organise some coffee and we passed a pleasant afternoon in Fatos's office. He was something of a raconteur. His eyes bulged, his hands shaped the air, and an unending smile lit the tops of his teeth. At one time he had been a journalist. Unfortunately his biografi was affected by his composer father's friendship with a director of broadcasting who was purged in the early seventies. Fatos was temporarily retired from his job at the newspaper and sent to work at the Elbasan metallurgy plant. Two years stretched to three, after his former newspaper employer would not take him back.

He left to work at a cement factory and spent all his spare time going from one Party office to another, trying to get his old job back. Finally he was given a chance as a children's-books editor. But even here was a potential minefield.

"Only fables about animals were acceptable. It had to be about the rabbit, or better still"—he laughed—"the 'collective of rabbits' who fought the big bad wolf."

Brikena had also started off in children's books, and one of her first tasks had been to plan a new edition of Grimm's fairy tales.

The problem was, she said, "fairy tales about kings, queens, and witches were not allowed to be published."

The book, like so many other politically dicey books, had been held up in production for eight years.

"Only, in this case, I was very glad for this to happen. You can imagine how an Albanian edition of Grimm's fairy tales would have read."

For a number of years Brikena and Fatos had been privileged readers of Western literature denied a wider audience. Fatos, with a great curve of smiling teeth protruding from his bottom lip, confessed to a great fondness for William Boyd.

"*An Ice-Cream War* I liked very, very much." He slapped his thigh and laughed at his memory of the silly, pompous English colonel.

Brikena blew another smoke ring at the ceiling and considered. Graham Greene's *The Comedians* she particularly liked. Greene's Haiti, she felt, very much resembled Albania.

"Now, this was one that nearly made it through to publication, but passages had to be left out because the biografis of the two lovers had made the editor-in-chief very nervous.

"You remember, there was the daughter of the Nazi and the son of the Communist. The affair might suggest that Communism and Nazism were on an equal footing.

"The editor-in-chief wanted the lover of the Communist to have a clean biografi."

I asked about Kadare, his standing, and the mere mention of his name had Fatos rock back in his chair and clap his hands.

"Kadare and William Boyd," he said. "I like both very much."

When Fatos was a teenager, it had been Kadare's poems that steered him towards literature.

"Unfortunately for me, around the time I was about to begin university Enver Hoxha gave a very important interview. He was asked, were he to have his life all over again, what career he would have chosen.

"Enver said, 'Why, I would like to be a mathematician. There can be no higher calling. A mathematician or a scientist.'

"This was devastating news," Fatos said, "because my father took me aside. And even though his background was in the arts he knew I would never be able to truly develop as a writer. 'Fatos,' he said, 'I think you should study mathematics.' "

Fatos laughed happily. There didn't seem to be any bitter memories.

"So," he said, "I became a very bad mathematician."

"Of course," I ventured, "some say Kadare was a propagandist." I mentioned *The Great Winter*, which Mimi's husband had roundly disdained. But Fatos knew both sides of the story.

"It's true," he conceded, "that he glorifies Hoxha, but you must know that if it were not for Hoxha, Kadare would have been crucified.

"I was a journalist at the time and there was talk among hardliners and the *sigourimi* that Kadare was at an end. This was true. He was in great danger.

"Of course Hoxha knew this—he was at Elbasan to open the metallurgy plant. A crowd had gathered, and quite unexpectedly a Party functionary stepped forth from the ranks of the workers to ask Hoxha's opinion of *The Winter of the Great Loneliness*. Did Comrade Enver think it worthy?

"Hoxha considered. He thought it was not a book to be 'lightly dismissed.' "

And here, Fatos held up a finger.

"In fact, he went further. He said, 'Of course, it has its faults, but Kadare is a good writer.' "

Fatos leant forward in his chair, his smiling teeth clenching his bottom lip.

"These words saved Kadare's life. Or, at the very least, saved him from prison." Fatos was sure of that.

"In the book, although Hoxha was glorified, socialism was directly attacked. Being intelligent as Kadare is—by attacking socialism in the Soviet Union he indirectly attacked socialism in Albania. But he could do this only by glorifying Hoxha. This was very clever."

The writers and critics held a meeting to debate the changes Kadare might make to his text. Hours of debate followed, from which there emerged a solitary change—*The Winter of the Great Loneliness* was shortened to *The Great Winter*.

I walked Brikena home. Her apartment was on the other side of the sprawling "black market" in the direction of Mt. Dajti.

It was already dark and the street was poorly lit. We had to feel our way over uneven ground. When we could, we walked along what we hoped was the centre of the road. Every so often the hooves of a horse and cart drew up behind—a driver mumbled a greeting—before the hooves melted into the night.

The biggest change since pluralism was the noise, said Brikena.

"All day long," she complained. "Buses, trucks, and the cars! It used to be so quiet."

Brikena and her husband, George, had moved into Brikena's mother's house. Brikena's linguist father had died some years ago, and an aunt had moved in to make up the numbers.

We walked around the back of a three-story building to the courtyard. Brikena said to look out for the oil crates, blackened wire boxes containing used oil bottles.

In total darkness we climbed three floors to the apartment, the comforts and imported tastes of which I hadn't expected. But then Brikena had spent a short period in Germany, and George, before marrying, had studied in France for five years. He was headed back there in another fortnight.

Brikena had warned me in advance that George was without any interest in politics. "George is a cynic." She told me this as we were climbing the stairs. If it was true, then this attitude struck me as a privileged sensibility. I thought back to Gjyzepina's poor brother-in-law with his dreams of France, and Clement's father's desperate pleas to various Party officials to tell him what he could do to improve his biografi. But I liked George. He had a big open face and was ready to laugh and kid around at the drop of a hat. We sat in the old linguist's book-lined study. There were comfortable armchairs and free-standing lamps.

I told George how plastic flowers had been glued to the dead wood of the shrub growing in the foyer of the Dajti, and he clasped his hands and started to recite the joke about the President and the Democrat leader being in each other's pocket.

Sali Berisha asks Ramiz: "Are you satisfied with all the terrible things I have been saying about you?"

And Ramiz answers: "No, no. Please, you must tell more!"

Brikena said disapprovingly, "George is not a serious person."

In Brikena's estimation this was a damning thing to say about anybody. I had noticed she wasn't comfortable laughing. A schoolgirl twittering emerged from the cool intellectual and she reacted as if she had been caught out, covering her face until she had regained control. Brikena was more comfortable tilting her head back and blowing smoke rings up to the ceiling. She did not wish anyone to think of her as being frivolous.

Brikena's mother, a tiny woman dressed entirely in black, had prepared a dish of delicious savouries wrapped in grape leaves. On a mantel was a photograph of her in the forties, as a partisan. She looked like Ginger Rogers in battle fatigues. The photograph had been taken in the mountains. Next to Brikena's mother another woman has a belt of ammunition slung over her shoulder. It seemed a happy occasion. The older woman took the photograph from her daughter's fingers and grinned at it for a moment.

I asked Brikena to ask her mother to tell us a little about her partisan experiences.

But Brikena answered for her. "I have asked her this many times and she always answers the same way."

"Yes?"

"She says it was like being in a film. A movie. It happened, and then you wondered if it had."

The vivacious young woman in the photograph stood up unsteadily. George took hold of her arm while she corrected a troublesome knee. She gathered up the dishes and carried them out to the kitchen, where there was some excited chatter, no doubt the aunt wanting to know what had been said, and then hoots of laughter.

19

I had been in Albania only ten days, and already Bill's appetites were fast becoming my own. I couldn't afford the dollar restaurant in the Dajti. The worst time was at night, when, even if I wasn't particularly hungry, eating and drinking were the only things to do. Sometimes I caught a glimpse through the dining-room doors of the sparkling array of beer and wine glasses, and of Bill and the aid workers sawing up lettuce and mayonnaise and braised cutlets which had been flown in from Italy.

For a handful of leks a vendor in the park opposite the hotel dropped a copper scoop into a sackful of blackened sunflower seeds, which is what the half-starved soldiers nibbled in their hands all day long. Sometimes I unwrapped the cake from Nick's mother and stared at the yellow oblong, until I thought better of it and returned the cake to its newspaper wrapping.

Some of the lek cafés offered beer, which came in small brown bottles without labels. But it had missed some vital stage in production. It tasted yeasty and bitter, and was undrinkable.

Hungarian chocolate from a white-coated woman who had set up shop in a kind of plastic igloo in the park usually kept me going through the day.

The artists and writers' building had a café downstairs.

Brikena had taken me there. It had the atmosphere of an old hunting lodge. Wooden tables with red tablecloths covered in cigarette burns were spread over a rambling ground floor and mezzanine area. A few tables were occupied by figures hunched in conversation. But there was nothing to eat or drink. They had run out of coffee late the previous afternoon.

Another café, Hungarian-owned, had started up across the road from the writers' building. Every day it drew sightseers to its doors. Faces pressed against the window in quiet awe of the shiny chrome and plastic surfaces inside. You sat in there eating small, sweet cakes and tried to prevent yourself from looking up at the drawn faces and salivating mouths at the window.

This morning I manage to get the table just beyond the end of the window. It is the only table that is humanely possible to eat at, but you still get to hear the odd slap and thump of a hand and shoulder against the plate-glass window.

A solidly built Hungarian minds the door, opening it just wide enough to let patrons through. His job is to identify paying customers and snatch them from the ragged mob on the pavement. There is a mad scramble, and the customers, like peas from a pod, are expectorated through the narrow angle of the doorway. We all arrive inside the beautiful shining chrome bar the same way, slightly dishevelled from the rough handling. Women bend down to recover their handbags and personal effects from the floor, and pat down their hair.

And this is how Munz arrives, lurching through the

door, his eyes wide with disbelief, like a freshly hooked fish. The bright imported lights catch the beady perspiration beneath his eyes while he fumbles around for his glasses.

"Well," he says, still breathing hard as he sits down. "I have a very big surprise for you."

He reaches inside his coat and slaps a tatty old envelope on the table.

"It's him. Shapallo."

"He's alive?"

"Yes, of course. I must say I am very glad to have been proven wrong. Perhaps," he says, "you will still get to meet our friend."

I start to ask him half a dozen questions at once until he shuts me up.

"I cannot tell you how sorry I am to have to admit this. For some months I have had a notice of a registered letter waiting for me at the Postal and Telegrams Office. I never thought for a moment . . . Well, I thought perhaps it is something from Germany. But Shapallo? No. Never." Then, rather sheepishly, Munz confesses to having misplaced the notice.

He apologises again. "I am very sorry to have to admit to this."

He pushes the letter across the table. "Please. You may read it."

20

Shapallo had simply and unhelpfully written his address as Gjaza. I couldn't find a trace of it on Cliff's map. It didn't mean anything to Bill, either.

"Wait until I check it out at the office. We have some different maps there," he said. In the afternoon he returned with a map identifying the exile camps in the south, and there was Gjaza, near Lushnje.

Shapallo's letter was more helpful in answering other matters. It seems Munz had got it wrong. Far from being thrown from the truck by the refugees, Shapallo had lost his nerve.

Somewhere along the road to Durrës his truck had blown a tyre. The refugees were told to get out of the truck and wait on the side of the road. And while the spare was being fitted, Shapallo had wandered away from the carousel of lights.

In the letter he speaks of being "drawn back into the night."

Munz could only speculate there. He had taken off his glasses and thought about it in the café for the moment, not seeing the hordes pressed and smudged against the window. He thought that perhaps Shapallo's age had something to do with it.

"The way old people wander off from nursing homes and lose their way." He shrugged. "I don't know. It is very curious. He was so eager to get away."

For the next two nights Shapallo had wandered across the coastal marshland. Gjaza, by the sound of it, had simply lain in his way.

The letter spoke of his stumbling on some farm buildings. A barn, I imagine. In the pitch black of night he clawed at a timber siding until a door gave way. In the letter Shapallo describes his "blindman's walk"—with outstretched hands he got no farther than three paces. Then he dragged his hands down the wall to a metal bed frame with springs, which he fell upon with total abandonment.

In the morning he took stock of his bearings. It was a stone floor. Other than the bed there were no furnishings. He walked to the window. The sun had risen half an inch above the horizon and there were men and women in blue uniforms digging trenches across a field of grey mud.

The letter mentions at length an odd little domestic detail, as if his discovery that he had left a trail of mud from the door to the bed suggests some larger truth. Shapallo confesses to suddenly feeling overcome by housekeeping anxiety. He describes his finding a stick and scraping the mud out the door; and then, straightening up, his eye travels across the marshland to the coast and for the first time he begins to entertain thoughts of staying on.

Four of us are to travel to Lushnje. Brikena for one, and her friend Zerena, another editor at the Naim Frasheri. Brikena has been magnificent. Her neighbour, Mentor, will drive us. Furthermore, her uncle, who lives in Lushnje, is expecting us. She has also rustled up a translator, a schoolteacher she knows from university days. For the first time in a while the cards seem to be falling right.

Lushnje is an easy hour-and-a-half drive. All the same, we meet nice and early in the courtyard at the Naim Frasheri, and while we are waiting for Mentor to fill up the tank, we slip into the café by the ground-floor bookshop.

Everyone is depressed by last night's news that Sali Berisha is withdrawing his Democrats from the governing coalition. Berisha cited irreconcilable differences, among them the Socialists' reluctance to arrest Nexhmije and put her on trial and Ramiz's refusal to bring the election date forward.

The marshland mentioned by Shapallo in his letter stretches from the coastline south of Durrës to the small, rolling hills that stay with us all the way to Lushnje.

We're travelling in the comparative luxury of an old beat-up Volvo, which Mentor's nephew sent him from Italy. "I am not ashamed to say this," he says. "But for forty-five years I work, and for what? My nephew escapes to Italy, and after a few months' work has enough for this beautiful car."

"He is very reliable," Brikena assured me. "Some of them, I can tell you, are madmen. They think they can drive, when in fact . . ."

Mentor's technique lies at the other end of the spectrum from Teti's. We rabbit-hop out of Tirana in fourth gear at twenty kilometres an hour.

Brikena tosses her head back and expels a mouthful of smoke, as the first of the countryside rolls by.

"It's so good to get out of the city. So good," she says, and I look back to see what I can make of Tirana, growing lower and lower in the rear mirror, now a footprint at the bottom of Dajti. It's hard to escape the feeling that Brikena's city weariness has been acquired from some other place.

Within half an hour we're at the Durrës turnoff, to head south. Just beyond the fork are scores of Italian lorries parked in a compound behind barbed wire. There is no other traffic, and because of this, one expects to come across a road barrier any moment. Or to be overhauled by an official grey van and flagged down.

It is hard to conclude anything at all about the passing landscape. It is obviously untenanted and, for that matter, unwanted. The marshland is only a few feet above sea level. From the road you can sense its edge and the proximity of the beach.

From one of Cliff's photographs taken at Durrës I seem to recall the beach being white and sandy and deserted but for Cliff, its only idler, with his out-of-season paleness, and I remember feeling in the photo the undeniable privilege of being there.

Harry Hamm's visit to the beach in Durrës thirty years earlier found it almost deserted. He had stayed at the Adriatic Hotel and describes coming down to breakfast one morning and finding at a table two Americans having the news in the Party newspaper *Zeri I Popullit* read to them. "The Americans," Hamm noted, "took noticeable pains to avoid contact . . ."

The Americans lay on the beach. The woman rubbed oil into the man's back. And later, the woman's shrieks of delight carried emptily and went unheeded as she was chased from the water by the man pretending to be a shark. The woman ran up the beach—like a Crusoe figure arriving at a deserted world.

In Sarandë, Hamm caught up with them. In the hotel register he found their words of praise for the socialist reconstruction attributed to an "American Workers Delegation."

———

A dark loam replaces the sand as the road bends inland from the coast.

By the roadside, tree stumps have been bitten and chewed down by men wielding axes for wood chips to fire their stoves.

To see these woodchip barometers down so low is an ominous sight—a few of the trunks are level with the ground and we are still to face the brute cold of winter.

In another thirty minutes we are at Kavajë.

Until now Kavajë had not reckoned in my thoughts or plans. But Zerena, it is, who casually mentions: "You should know that this town is known throughout Albania. Official cars couldn't pass through here without their windows being smashed."

"This is true," says Mentor. "In Kavajë you gave the Democrat sign or you didn't get through."

In dribs and drabs Kavajë's brave defiance is established. Mentor's foot has lifted off the gas and we're back to bunny-hopping, our heads and necks jerking comically in opposite directions. We stall, finally and appropriately, while Zerena is explaining a soccer match which sparked the public demonstrations against the regime. And there, in the main street, without fear of obstructing traffic, Mentor lights a cigarette and adds what he can to Zerena's account.

"The match was between Kavajë and the Minister of the Interior's side," Zerena thought. "The crowd did not like the referee's decisions and became very, very angry."

Mentor is less certain. "There was a soccer match," he says. "This is a fact. But I do not recollect the referee in this . . ."

"Perhaps I am wrong about the referee," says Zerena. "But what is also a fact is after the game the crowd threw the works of Enver Hoxha onto the soccer field."

"Ah that, yes," agrees Mentor. "Kavajë is a very brave town."

Zerena, who has been watching me take down notes, asks, "You are interested in Kavajë?"

The reason she asks is that she is a friend of the director of the nail factory. "He can tell you everything," she says.

The Volvo croaks back to life, and within a few minutes we draw up at the gates of the nail factory. Zerena asks that we wait. She will go and find Riza and perhaps, as Zerena calls it, we will have "an exchange."

In a few minutes she returns with a big smile. At her elbow is Riza Hoxha. The invitation is for coffee.

"There is time. In Albania it is the only thing that we have in abundance," jokes the director.

The nail factory, like every other factory in the country, has ground to a halt. With Riza is Sali Volgi, the director— up until two weeks ago.

Inside the gates we climb to an outside landing which is at eye level with the workers' flats and forests of TV aerials. The only noise in Kavajë, a town of twenty-eight thousand, belongs to the feathery cussacking of pigeons roosting in the gutterings and eaves of the surrounding white-bricked warehouses.

The factory café is empty and, like an old food safe, bare but for the crumbs and the lingering smell of food long since eaten. We sit at a table covered with a soiled oilskin cloth, and an old man in a white jacket brings a tray of coffee— and, surprisingly, an armful of oranges.

An element of formality and seriousness follows as I am bodily assisted from my chair and placed next to Sali. Happier with this new seating arrangement, he opens a small black folder in which he has recorded three months of rebellion in Kavajë, which earned it a reputation as something other than the place where nails are made.

21

On the afternoon of March 22, 1990, the students in Tirana hauled down the monolithic statue of Enver in Skanderbeg Square.

But in Kavajë, preceding the students' action by two or three hours, as Sali was quick to proudly point out, the busts of Enver were attacked and destroyed. Ramiz Alia's portrait, which had hung from the town's one set of traffic lights, was set on fire. In the nail factory workers placed a tyre around Enver's statue in the factory yard and set fire to it.

Three days later a soccer match drew a huge crowd to the stadium. Word had been given that at the conclusion of the soccer match everyone would stand and shout.

The Party Secretary for Kavajë, Agron Tafa, who was also a former vice-director of the Ministry of the Interior, was relying on his presence to have an intimidating effect. But immediately the game was over, and as Tafa prepared to leave, he was fearlessly baited by the crowd. Since Tafa had once been a horse-and-cart driver the football fans were shouting, "Hey, Agron, from cart driver you have become a shepherd!"

Then people began to chant and throw the works of Enver Hoxha onto the field. This was something new. Protests of this kind, of any kind for that matter, were unprecedented.

After this, Sunday matches were very well attended. A football crowd organises itself and enters the stadium with a frivolous spirit. It was Kavajë's only means of getting a crowd together without the risk of organising one.

The day after the soccer match at which Tafa was insulted, Kavajë witnessed its first demonstration. It was late afternoon and two hundred young men gathered near the Party Committee building. They had requested a favour from the electrical workers: not to switch on the streetlights until they were given the word. The demonstrators hid their faces with jackets and shouted for "freedom and democracy," and a chant went up comparing Enver with Hitler. Patriotic songs were sung, songs from the turn of the century, when the country was struggling out from under the Ottoman yoke. This went on for forty-five minutes. The demonstrators then moved off to the town centre, where still more young people gathered.

Inside the tiny apartments the boiling water was stilled on the Primus. Conversations stopped mid-sentence. People sat on the edge of their chairs, and inclined their good ear towards the windows. It was incredible. The people in the apartments exchanged glances. Nobody dared to speak. Those down in the street were chanting. And then it all ended, like a shower of rain that passes quickly over a city.

As soon as the protesters left the centre the lights came on, but nobody in the apartments dared to go out. Nobody could trust the silence. They waited, and their suspicions soon bore fruit, as they heard the tyres of police vans driving slowly through the empty streets.

Midnight, at an urgent meeting held at the Kavajë Party Headquarters, it was "officially" decided that the disturbance had been "caused by fifteen to twenty hooligans." Sali, attending in his capacity as the nail factory director, remembered the faces of alarm and their "lying to deceive themselves as much as the record." The Party Secretaries from different plants were instructed to educate the workers, and a small token price was exacted in the form of two arrests.

At the meeting Sali signalled his intention to resign from the Party.

"In March 1990 this was considered a dangerous action," he said. "They asked me to think it over."

By now, word of the Kavajë demonstrations had spread to Tirana and Shkodër and Elbasan. Sali travelled around the country. "Wherever I went," he said, "when people found out I was from Kavajë they were curious to know how the protest had been achieved."

The nail factory, which employed twelve hundred workers, had had its share of problems. For two years it had languished because of the shortage of materials. The economy was fast winding down. The metallurgy plant at Elbasan had stopped sending steel to Kavajë for nails, and this had led to nail workers being laid off without pay.

Sali sent off letters describing the problem to Party leaders in Tirana. There came no reply. He despatched more letters and telegrams until, finally, the Party leaders agreed to visit. Until this time no one had dared to contradict the official position that, in Albania, paradise had been achieved.

The Party sent Lenka Cuko, a former peasant who had risen through the ranks to become one of the dozen most important Politburo members, described by Sali as "a woman with an idiot's face and black eyes."

"The meeting was historic," he said. "If for no other reason than Lenka was accustomed to respect and she got none."

The meeting was held within a week of the protests at the stadium and outside Party Headquarters. Lenka was accompanied by another official, Muho Asllani, the first Party Secretary of the Durrës area. Sali explained the factory's problems, the difficulties the workers were having in trying to feed their families, and Lenka responded, "We have not come here with our pockets full of money."

The workers then detailed the food shortages—each worker was down to a cupful of milk a day.

"You need to understand," said Sali. "This was the first time workers had the courage to mention such things to Party leaders."

Officially all was rosy. Unofficially, the phrase on everyone's lips went Mish—ish—sh [Meat—none to eat—but don't repeat—only whisper].

One of the workers then asked Lenka, "Why don't you allow the people to have cows at home?"

"What!" reacted Lenka. "Do you want to turn Albania into the Soviet Union—a revisionist country?"

The workers grew more insistent. They began to put forward demands. At which point Lenka and Muho retreated, suggesting that the discussion had been sabotaged by "political enemies."

Further meetings with the "blockmen" followed, but

nothing was resolved, and the factory finally stopped working shortly after the meeting with Lenka.

From this moment the nail factory workers began to take things into their own hands.

A truck from Skrapar, a Communist stronghold in the south, which had arrived at the factory for nails, was hijacked. A number of younger workers took the truck and drove to the library, where they smashed the windows and loaded the truck with the works of Enver Hoxha, and a message for the driver: "This is what we have to give to the people of Skrapar—not nails."

Traffic from Gjirokastër, Enver's birthplace, was routinely stopped in town and the question asked of the drivers: "Who are you for—democracy or Enver?"

Summer was near and people started to crowd the beaches. Wary of the behaviour that had occurred in the soccer stadium, the Party sent uniformed police to watch over the bathers.

The rest of April, May, and June passed peacefully enough. But on July 8 the regime struck back. The *sampists*, highly paid shock troops of the Minister of Interior, arrived in Kavajë. In the afternoon they turned up at Golem Beach and went about their business. Men were beaten up and women stripped of their clothing and bathing suits. From the beach they rolled into town picking people off the street and locking them in their grey panel vans.

One who resisted was Josef Buda, twenty-one, who, standing with his fiancée at the entrance to town, was shot dead. The *sampists* took Buda's body to the centre of town and dumped it on the street.

The townspeople wrapped the body in a sheet and carried it to Buda's parents' house. The next day the funeral cortege outnumbered the entire population of Kavajë. The coffin, covered with the bloodstained sheet from the previous day, was borne through the streets by thirty thousand mourners. From the cemetery the funeral procession continued on to the Party Headquarters, where the mourners set fire to the building and set alight police cars and the cars of Party functionaries.

For a month afterwards, Kavajë was surrounded by tanks and police. For two months the *sampists* camped outside the town. By then, however, protests had broken out in all parts of the country—Shkodër, Tirana, Korcë, Elbasan. Everywhere the statues of Stalin and Hoxha were being smashed.

22

For all its efforts and heroism, Kavajë would appear to have benefitted very little. Before moving on to Lushnje we drove past the other big plant, a glass factory. Its windows had been smashed. The padlocks and chained gates had rusted and the stillness of the factory spoke of abandonment. The only place to have seen money spent on its construction recently was the newly built Party Headquarters.

While we were still in Kavajë, Brikena, in front with Mentor, suddenly twisted around and gazed longingly back to a horse-drawn cart.

"Milk!" she said. "I am sure that was milk."

South of Kavajë the road twists around hillsides planted in olive groves. From the air, according to Mentor, the trees have been grown so as to spell ENVER HOXHA.

A little farther on we meet up with the railway line, another triumph of the Albanian Youth, built back in the sixties and seventies. Here Zerena leans forward to point out "Shkurte Vata." The statue is of a young woman with her right arm raised, her hand balled up in a fist.

We roll slowly to a stop, not on the shoulder but where it is equally safe—in the middle of the road. Within minutes a goat dragging a cart has appeared. Some small children with shaven heads stare at us while we stare at the statue.

We leave Mentor stamping the cold from his feet on the road. A small bridge crosses the railway line built especially for pilgrims to sit at the heroine's feet. During the construction of the railway Shkurte had died after an embankment collapsed on her. Enver immediately seized on the tragedy for "photo opportunities." Newspapers showed him clasping the shoulders of Shkurte's father, a poor bewildered villager. Poetry was written about Shkurte. And in the ultimate of glories, she was made a member of the Party posthumously.

Until recently, Tirana Television started its nightly broadcasts with pictures of Shkurte Vata's statue. The musical accompaniment was a specially commissioned score.

Zerena says this changed only recently. Her husband,

Palli, a cameraman, was asked to film sky. Nowadays the programmes start with a vapid blue sky and the national anthem.

Lushnje begins promisingly enough with a decorative line of palm trees on the outskirts of the town. So unexpected, so persuasively cheerful are the palms that they almost deny Lushnje's reputation as the "capital of concentration camps."

The best view of Lushnje is to be had from the restaurant on the hilltop overlooking town. It is called Blerimi, "the blooming flower." From up there the eye seeks out the coastline, which on the map lies another forty or fifty kilometres to the west. To the naked eye the horizon is lost in a mauve-coloured paste: Italy is rumoured to lie in that direction.

The official view, also obtained from the Blerimi, takes in the Myzeqe, in better years a checkerboard of maize and wheat, the food bowl of Albania, but at this time of the year it is uniformly tan.

The other thing to note is what appear to be clusters of dark rock dotting the Myzeqe. These are settlements—officially, state farms. Alternatively, they are camps, exile camps, stunted bits of city that have been relocated to the flat countryside. Even here, for all its abundant space, the regime has insisted that "one family's floor is another family's ceiling," and as in the city, the crude Stalinist housing models have been replicated.

As we enter Lushnje, standing beneath the last palm tree is an old man in an overcoat. Mentor pulls over, presumably to ask directions. Then, inexplicably, everyone gets out of the car.

Brikena kisses the stranger on both cheeks.

"This is Doctor Cabey. My uncle. He has lived here all his life."

Brikena's uncle has nothing much to add to this. We shake hands and he returns his hands to his overcoat and we start over the road to a line of three-storey apartments. We follow the doctor around to the back of the building, across a scruffy yard. Chickens peck over a stony ground. A vile black smoke blowing across the yard without neighbourly concern is apparently from the bakery.

We trudge up the stairs behind her uncle, to a tiny apartment. The doctor and his wife share the apartment with an adult son, who Brikena had warned me would be very keen to practise his English on me. He turns out to be an anaemic boy with a gravel rash over his chin which I suspect could be cleared up with a good soapy wash. Somehow he has acquired a tape of Talking Heads and is anxious for assurances that, in the West, Talking Heads are held in high esteem.

He fondles the tape and I tell him what I can.

In reply he repeats his one and only incantation. "David Byrne. He is very, very good, I think. Yes?"

The doctor's wife—Mrs. Cabey, I suppose it is, since she is never introduced—has prepared a table. There are sawn loaves of dark Albanian bread, goat cheese, and olives marinated with peppers and oil. The toilet, I discover, is in the kitchen, a longdrop unceremoniously sited before the stove so that the doctor's wife has to lean over the gaping porcelain hole to move the pots about the Primus stove.

She agrees, "It is a very small house." They had had the opportunity of a larger apartment on the lower floor but turned it down. "We worried that our conversations might be overheard from the street, that we would be overheard and put in prison," she says.

Soon Brikena's friend, the English teacher, arrives. A broad-shouldered, handsome man in his mid-thirties with a high glistening forehead, Kadris is immaculately turned out in white collar and tie, a suit "from abroad," and polished black shoes. He appears to be, as Brikena might put it, "a serious man."

He begins on a humble note, apologising for his English. To my ear it sounds fine, every bit as good as Brikena's.

"This is the first time that I use it on a native speaker of English. Up until now I have a very good reputation for speaking the language."

We sit down to eat, and throughout the meal the doctor says little, even to Brikena. Some vital cord broke in him long ago. He listens and confirms another's viewpoint with a nod, or purses his lips together to indicate a difference.

Kadris is anxious to know of reaction in Tirana to the Democrats' withdrawal from government. Sali Berisha's actions have disappointed him.

"Better to dance with the devil you know," he says. "The Socialists can do anything now."

The doctor clears his throat and everyone looks his way expectantly, as if to will him on. He has something to say about the corrupting effect of power, and offers this epiphany: "Wherever you go in the world the political leaders are the same. The grapes see each other and ripen."

The doctor's refuge, I discover, is his study, a tiny world of white pillows, medical texts, texts on semiotics by Brikena's late father, and stuffed birds, of which there are too many to count. Stout-chested birds with glass eyes, which the doctor has glued onto plastic branches. Small birds, field tinkers, long-legged birds from the marshes—all of them stuffed and without song.

I had thought of going directly to Gjaza, but by the time we have finished up at the doctor's it has become dark. I say goodbye to Brikena and Zerena and watch the Volvo grow small in the distance, beyond the last palm tree. Kadris mentions that the leader of the Lushnje Democrats is waiting to meet me: Kutjim Gina. The doctor's last duty will be to hand me over to "Mister Gina."

We wander through town, past the hotel and the adjoining café, and as we pass, a quick glance in the window reveals the Lushnje menfolk in British Telecom jerseys. Men lined up at the espresso machine, others sitting around the tables—in dark blue ribbed jerseys. It suddenly occurs to me that Don might be staying at the same hotel.

It is five minutes' walk to the Democratic Party Headquarters, a chapel-size building. A steep goat track straggles up a small rise above the deserted marketplace.

Kutjim Gina has been waiting for us. He is a wiry man with snow-white hair above a tanned face rutted with worry lines. Kadris tells me that Mister Gina used to be an economics professor, and this is a surprise, because he doesn't look as if he has spent a single working day inside.

Best of all, Mister Gina has been apprised of our plans. Arrangements have been made. The Democratic Party car, a gift from the government when pluralism was introduced, will be at our disposal.

"You may go to Gjaza. You may go wherever you wish."

With the arrival of the car, Mister Gina had explored parts of the Myzeqe he hadn't known to exist.

He takes my notebook and writes down the names of the camps near here—Gradishte, Savra, Rrapes sector, Grabiau, Plyk, Dushkt. He writes down the number of families in each. To Tchermë, he adds "Tchermë immigrants"—these are poor souls who have sought out the camps for a better life.

We part company with the doctor, who assures me that with Mister Gina I'm in the best possible hands, and we watch him poke his walking stick distrustfully ahead of himself down the goat track, heading home, back to his silent world of stuffed birds.

23

When the Lushnje chapter of the Democratic Party formed at Mister Gina's house on January 3, 1991, it was decided by all those in attendance that democracy's first duty would be to restore truth-telling, that from this point on "an orange would be, in fact, an orange." And an apple would return to being an apple and "not a creation of Enver Hoxha."

Mister Gina said it was well known that the Party of Labour was in crisis. "They forced the people to attend their meetings. These meetings were filmed." The next day they would ask, "Please, tell us why you did not applaud at the meeting?" Sometimes they paid people to applaud at meetings, and sometimes people applauded "because they needed the money or else they were afraid of losing their jobs."

The day after the local chapter of the Democratic Party formed in Lushnje, with Mister Gina installed as its leader, twenty-two thousand people had poured into Lushnje Square. They were, in large part, political exiles who had swarmed out of the backwaters of the Myzeqe to hear of their new freedom. At least they were free now in the technical sense. Those who still had homes in other parts of the country were free to return to them, but this freedom extended only to those exiled in the last ten years. For the rest, those generations born to the camps had no other place to return to. They were free, but in the material sense nothing was about to change. For the moment, however, freedom as an abstract idea was intoxicating.

People wept and applauded, and those who raised the Democrat salute were later identified in film taken by the sigourimi and arrested. Perversely, sixty people who had walked to Lushnje to hear of their freedom ended up being arrested for responding inappropriately.

Since that time Mister Gina had travelled to every camp in the Myzeqe. He knew their inhabitants. He had met with every exile. Their biografis were all known to him.

"They are all Democrats," he said.

Mister Gina insisted on inspecting my room in the one and only hotel. He wanted to satisfy himself that I would be comfortable.

On the stairs Kadris confirmed for me: "There are no other English staying in the hotel."

We followed a girl with a torch up the stairs into the dark recesses of the hall. A smell of sewage grew nearer. Other women hotel workers emerged along the dark walls, unhurried.

We came to my room. Mister Gina elbowed ahead and tried the light—with the inevitable result. He sent the young girl off, and until she returned with a bulb from another room I stood with Mister Gina clicking his tongue like a locust.

After a long silence the girl came back. She shone the torch at the ceiling. Mister Gina climbed onto a chair and replaced the bulb, and the light came on.

"Perfect," I said.

Unfortunately there is no flush or running water, except between the hours of 3 and 6 a.m. I discovered this at 7 a.m., and more alarming, I traced the evil smell in the hall to a tide of raw sewage which had risen from the bowls of the communal toilets just two doors away from my room.

My window gives onto a courtyard filled with rubble and debris and, quite improbably, an old Russian lorry propped up on bricks and trapped by walls on all four sides. This morning, when I pull the curtain back, a silver-haired man in an officer's uniform full of sharp creases is slowly mounting the steps to the outside landing. He looks a forlorn figure. He walks with his head down, and behind his back, in his hands, he carries a pair of white parade-ground gloves.

24

From the carpark of the Blerimi you can see a road straight as a needle laid across the plain. It is the road to Fier and in this direction we carry on for about twenty minutes, before pulling off onto a loose metal road and heading south.

Mister Gina explains the countryside as we pass through it. Some of it has been sown in cotton. Most of it lies unsown. Here is Krutje, the first cooperative farm in Albania and the model on which others were built, a watery maze of sticks and hanging plastic and low-lying buildings. A woman in a plastic raincoat walks a farm track carrying a large fish.

In Kavajë I'd heard it mentioned that Lenka was from here.

"Lenka, so you've heard?" says Mister Gina. He is evidently pleased.

We drive on without further landmarks, and the deepening isolation is measured by every pothole along the road.

By the time we turn off into a muddy track which brings us to Gjaza, we are no farther than forty minutes' drive from Lushnje.

The track into Gjaza ends in a ditch and fields. Three-storey apartment blocks stand to one side of the track. On the other side is the old Albania to which the exiles have been banished. Hidden underneath trellises of grapevines are tiny whitewashed huts, and from here mobs of tiny, grubby-faced children swarm out to greet us. Following at their rear are the parents—the men in blue cotton pants and jackets. The women come to the doors of the huts to see what the fuss is all about.

Right away I find myself looking around for a tall, stooped figure with a scarred forehead.

Children tug at my jeans and laugh. A short man with a dark pudding bowl of hair is shaking hands with me. Sali Agolli introduces his brother, Xhelaodin, and the next thing I'm being propelled down a garden path to their hut. I glance back to see Kadris holding up his trouser legs so the cuffs don't get muddied.

An old woman dressed in black cotton orders us inside. This is Asie, the elderly mother of Sali and Xhelaodin. She is impatient for us to pass through her doorway and is shouting at her sons to get us in here. This morning the temperature must be near freezing and the old woman has just finished washing and swabbing down her stone floors.

Kadris is doing his best to bring this momentum to a halt. The older brother, Sali, has taken my hand in his, while he listens intently to Kadris. The old woman starts up again, but this time the son raises his hand to silence her. The mother catches my eye and touches a cup to her lips and laughs. She beckons me inside, but at that moment Kadris pulls me back the other way.

"This man, Shapallo," Mister Agolli wishes to ask, "is he an exile, here in Gjaza? What height is he?" Mister Agolli gazes up at me, politely intent, but there is a discouraging lack of light in those eyes.

I start to describe the high forehead and the pleasant countenance of the statues. A very tall man—they nod. But the bit about film-star looks and excellent teeth is lost on them.

The Agolli brothers would like to help, I can see that. They listen to Kadris's description. Sali scratches his chin and glances at his younger brother, who draws a line down his forehead. He leaves his finger there and for the moment watches me, and then it all sinks in. Sali rocks his head back. He speaks excitedly with his brother and then Kadris is tipping me through the doorway out of the old woman's grasp. The two brothers have hurried ahead. We leave the garden and walk to the end of the muddy track.

When I stop, the kids following behind crash into the backs of my legs. Kadris places a hand on two heads and with a few gentle words the children stay put and watch as we pick our way across the ploughed rock-hard fields.

Ahead of us, the tails of Sali's cotton jacket flap up and down over a back which is raw with cold.

About one hundred metres of open field separate us from a tiny whitewashed hut all on its own. Sali arrives ahead of us and throws the door wide and stands there with an arm extended, like a real-estate agent. There is the faint smell of recent habitation and a sprinkling of hay over the floor, but no Shapallo.

He was here as recently as one month ago. Since then he had moved to Savra, a collection of brick buildings we passed on our way here, a few kilometres outside Lushnje. There are tiny scrapings on the wall above the bed. I move in for a closer look at the word "Petra." The name of Sali's pet goat.

He was nine years old when he scratched the name against the wall. The Agollis had been exiled from Peshkopi when the state needed victims as examples of what happened to those who opposed collectivisation. They were declared "by the will of the peasants" to be class enemies.

For ten years, the five-strong Agolli family had bedded down on the floor each night. In time they had received permission to build their present hut and, after working in the fields all day, worked at night to build their new house out of mud bricks.

After the family moved, the hut was used for storing winter feed. When Shapallo moved in, there was a little hay scattered over the floor. Another two months and he would have found the old bed frame buried under with winter feed stacked to the door.

In July the maize stood tall as a man's midriff, and leading up to harvest heads like those belonging to swimmers nodding out beyond the breakers moved through the yellow maize. Sali told how as a child he had watched the adults' towering height above the maize being gradually whittled down as the maize grew taller and humbled its masters. The maize started out from under the soles of their feet and grew like a malignant weed until it had reapportioned the world. Late in summer it was cut down and the grey soil re-emerged. A natural cycle. And much like a tide which sweeps back and forth, maize had its own wandering instincts, changing the colours of Gjaza from yellow to grey and the depth of the land that was traversed, daily, from shoulder to ankle height, back and forth, a shifting colour and texture.

The maize was at shoulder height the morning Shapallo made his appearance; and not since childhood, that Sali could remember, had a figure so dominated the maize at this time of the year.

There was no fuel for the tractors and threshers, so they were using scythes and moving through the maize swinging the scythe from left to right, occasionally standing up to relieve a crick in the lower back. On one of these occasions Sali had straightened up in time to see "a man drowning" at the edge of the field, as Shapallo, with flailing arms, fell headlong into the crop.

They assumed he was a highlander. But for all his height, the highlander was light as a feather. Sali and his brother carried Shapallo inside the hut and laid him out on the rusted springs of the bed frame.

A cup of water from the spring dribbled over his chin. After a while Shapallo came round. He tried to sit up but his elbows fell out from under him like matchsticks.

The Agollis and the rest of the exiles hadn't known what to make of Shapallo. At another time, during the seventies, they would have assumed he was a spy. But it had quickly become obvious that he knew nothing about livestock or horticulture. He appeared to have the manners of someone from the city, but no one could be sure about that, either, other than those perhaps with long memories.

He did not eat ravenously. Another exile gave Shapallo a precious egg. To the astonishment of the exiles, the highlander nibbled at the cap, and then, for reasons of either exertion or taste, pushed the rest aside and sipped water with a mint leaf.

A chair was found for the stranger and Shapallo spent his mornings sitting in the sun at the edge of the fields. He grew stronger. But at night the exiles were kept awake by a terrible hacking cough.

A fortnight passed. Shapallo grew strong enough to collect his own water from the spring.

Soon after this he had turned up at the Agollis' door to ask for work.

The fields had entered a new cycle and the yellow straw had already been cut away from the earth. Small fires had to be lit, and the earth split and opened up. They worked with shovels and picks in a line which moved mechanically across the field, and Shapallo, despite his advancing years, kept up.

They tilled the fields—got everything ready. Then one day the brigadier walked across the field to tell them they had no fertiliser or seed. The exiles dropped their shovels and walked silently back to their huts.

Since late September, Gjaza had waited expectantly for the onset of winter. The Agollis were waiting to see what the regime would do next, whether they would be left to starve. September passed. October, November they waited. The exiles picked their small plots of grapes and made raki. They tended the odd farm beast, a cow or a goat. Children in rags and bare feet pushed unwilling cows across the mud to the roadside grasses. Everyone waited to see what winter would bring.

Word soon arrived in Gjaza that foreigners had reached Lushnje. A tall man was handing out blue jerseys. Children were posted at the roadside, outside Gjaza, to watch for the man bearing jerseys.

Another rumour spoke of the Red Cross taking food, clothing, and medicine to the exiles in Savra. The aid was selective. Everything was going to the exiles.

It was medicine that Shapallo needed most. He waited

for the aid to arrive, and while he waited the nights grew longer and colder and his cough grew worse. Each morning the younger Agolli brother went to the hut expecting to raise a grey blanket over a corpse.

Late October, the nights had become so bad for Shapallo that he couldn't wait any longer. One fine morning he had set out to walk to Savra to present himself to the foreigners. That had been six weeks ago, and there had been no word of him since.

In Gjaza, at least one other exile was waiting anxiously to hear back from her old backgammon partner.

25

The small oil heater gives off a smell stronger than its heat. In Gjaza there is no wood. There is electricity but no heaters.

Frieda apologises for her hoarseness. Her forehead is damp with sweat—for days she has been stuck with a cold.

From somewhere she has found some lipstick. She has on a smart suede jerkin and a lovely cream jersey spun with natural wool—which is perhaps what she would have worn had her old life been allowed to proceed. Frieda attended primary school in Italy, a French college in Austria. She comes from a wealthy Catholic family and was well-travelled at an early age. Italy. Vienna. She lived in a house with high walls, carpeted rooms with tall windows and silver trays. For the last twenty years, however, she has worked as a seamstress for two dollars a month.

Little of the exile's life would appear to have rubbed off on her spirit. There is nothing bitter in her face. There is none of that heavy-heartedness that has made Doctor Cabey such a figure of despair. In the doctor's study Frieda would be the plover, chesty, spirited.

On the way to Frieda's hut Kadris told me that she was a doctor's daughter and that sometimes she used to play backgammon with Shapallo. But I can't very well go straight to the point of discussing Shapallo. Mister Gina also knows of Frieda. He said her family held some kind of record for the number of years spent in prison and exile. At such times I noticed Frieda's name mentioned—not with pity as much as with awe.

In 1946 her father was arrested and his private clinic in Tirana was confiscated. He was released after three months, but his impertinence in asking for his property to be returned brought him ten years in jail.

Another branch of Frieda's family had fought in the mountains against the Communists, and from these cousins she had inherited bad biografi.

Her biografi also revealed that her family had lived near the French consulate in Tirana, and during the time of the Zog regime the French consul had been a family friend.

In 1949 Frieda was accused of working for the French Secret Service and sentenced to fifteen years in prison. She was still in prison when, in 1954, her mother was released without a place or a home to go to. One of the old family servants tried to take her in, but the regime intervened, and she was thrown out in the street and left to sleep in churches and beg for bread.

———

Frieda leans forward, she taps my notebook. She says, "My mother's name is Marta Doda."

In 1960 Frieda joined her father in Lushnje, where he had been sent to work. Although she was forbidden to leave the town, the sixties were Frieda's only years of freedom since she was a girl.

In the early seventies she was picked up in another sweep through the country's biografis. She leans forward with the date the way she had when she supplied her mother's name—"July 6, 1972."

Without warning the police arrived at her door and told her to get her things together. She asked where she was being sent to. The police shrugged. They said it was none of their concern.

She asked then if she could say goodbye to her father, who by this time was blind and ill.

The police said, "What does this mean? We do not understand 'goodbye.' "

Frieda was thrown in the police van and driven to Gjaza. Two months later, she received word that her father had died.

"Now," she says, smiling brightly, "what would you like to know about Shapallo?"

"Well, anything. What did he tell you about himself?"

"You must know this yourself, that he had been an actor, yes. He mentioned some difficulties . . ."

I asked to see the backgammon board, and she laughed.

"There is no backgammon board! We had to imagine a board. One thing you must understand, exiles have nothing if they don't have memories."

Frieda told me about a journey she had made as a newly pardoned exile back to her old neighbourhood. She travelled with friends to Tirana, where she discovered that her old house had passed on to the Minister of the Interior.

She knocked on the door, and a teenage girl answered. The Minister's daughter reluctantly stepped aside for Frieda and her exile friends.

Frieda looked in at the guest room, then the sitting room. She noticed the changes. The sitting room, for example, had been divided. The Minister's daughter asked how she knew the house so well. Frieda calmly told her, "This is my house."

The teenager tried to frighten Frieda by reminding her that her father was the Minister of the Interior.

"Then she asked me, if this was indeed my house, then why had I left it . . . ?

"I had to explain to this girl, the Minister's daughter, that I had been in exile.

"Then she asked me for proof that the house was mine. I showed her the documents and she became very frightened. It was a wonderful moment."

Frieda says, "According to the law I will get my house back. The Parliament decided that all confiscated property would be returned to the owners from before the war.

"You will be returning to Tirana. Will you please tell the Minister of the Interior that we are long overdue in switching houses. Tell him I am ready to give him my cot in Gjaza. I have been here twenty years—it is enough."

And she laughed, a wonderful smoker's laugh.

It is time we were under way. Mister Gina has booked a table at the Blerimi. But as we make our way from Frieda's, men in blue cotton uniforms come to the edge of bamboo fences. Or else with blank faces they stand in our path, and we are held up with more stories, still more biografi.

One man wants to tell me that he was expelled from school nearly forty years ago for laughing. "It was the day Stalin died, but I had no idea. None of us knew," he says plaintively. "I happened to be laughing at a boy with a hole in his pants. I knew nothing about Stalin at that moment. I was nine years old."

Another whose face is horribly disfigured with sores suppurating with pus and black cancerous growths presents himself as a "freedom fighter." He is so repulsively ugly that I cannot bear to look at him. Politely I take down his details as Kadris supplies them—until the older Agolli brother and Mister Gina drag me away to the car, and Kadris, after conferring with Sali, says the man is a spy.

"A weak character," says the older Agolli, bowing in the window. "He will stay. He has no place to go. No other life. As the camp population goes down he will remain to the last."

"And you?"

"My friend, every day we stay here reminds us of the past. But along with this spy we have no place to go to, either."

26

Mister Gina had booked a table. He had had in mind a special lunch in the upstairs room of the Blerimi, but clearly the reservation has slipped the minds of management.

Puddles lay over the floor, and through a broken pane in the door leading out to a patio a cold wind was blowing. The tablecloths hadn't been changed in days.

So we popped back downstairs to where a kind of warmth collected among the smoke and the close-set shoulders and chairs pressed together. Down here we huddled, and the raki took instant effect. As Kadris remarked, "The sun shone most brilliantly on our insides."

Kadris was in a better mood now. The interpreting and endless translation at Gjaza had left him exhausted. Towards the end of our time with Frieda he had grown impatient, snapping his replies when asked to repeat something or to help with disentangling a muddled sentence, which was often hazy and jammed just like the pictures Albania had received of the outside world.

"When we first came here we had to help drain the swamp of bodies."

And while Frieda smiled moistly, Kadris, hunch-shouldered, with his hands rammed home deep in his coat pockets, had swung his knees around and snapped, "Boulders. I said 'boulder'!"

"Boulder?"

"Boulders!"

It was an exhausting business, which had contributed to the silence during the drive back to Lushnje. Mister Gina smoked a cigarette meditatively in the front, and in the back Kadris leant away from me, his head inclined towards the window to discourage my asking questions.

No one had said anything until about ten minutes out from Lushnje, when the driver announced, "Savra."

In the dim light some women were digging a trench in a field. A muddy track ran down one side of it and there was just time enough to catch a glimpse of the familiar reddish buildings at the end of it. I would have liked to stop and have a look around. But Kadris closed his eyes. Mister Gina blew smoke at the road ahead. And the driver's foot fell upon the accelerator pedal with renewed purpose.

We ate hungrily from a plate of schnitzel and cold chips, peppers and onions, and for the first time I found myself divining the gentler properties of raki, which reminded me of pastis and liquorice.

In the declining light and through the misted windows the view of the Myzeqe softened, and with it the view of the hills outside distant Fier dissolved to darkness.

Kadris was pointing out the window, and rather futilely I was searching the murk for the distant hilltop, for the Ardenice Monastery, where Kadris had worked as a tourist guide. It wasn't a job that he had actively sought.

"One day I was told I would no longer be required to teach literature. I was asked to be a guide. Usually," he said, "this was not a job to fall to someone of my biografi." Contact with foreigners was considered a perk, like access to good food and good wine.

"And you should know," he added, "the restaurant was the best in all of Albania. Absolutely the best. This is so. But at the same time the job held many risks. Many, many risks."

On clear days, he said, looking south from the hilltop one can see the oil wells.

"The foreigners would ask me, 'Please, Kadris, will you tell me, what are those tall constructions in the distance?'

"Of course, I could not say, 'Those are oil wells.' Somebody might overhear and I would be accused of betraying state secrets.

"So naturally, I would answer: 'Please, what constructions? I do not see anything but the beautiful Myzeqe.'"

He rested a hand on his glass, as if to steady himself. "All my life I have lived in Lushnje. No one ever mentioned these labour camps."

By the time we motored down the hill from the Blerimi the main street of Lushnje was deserted, the café below the hotel was closed, and the only person out was Doctor Cabey's son. We had to stop and wind down the window to receive the limp handshake of the Talking Heads fan.

He was well. We were well. And we carried on.

Kadris said the job of looking after the restaurant and hotel food supplies for Lushnje had fallen to the doctor's son; the job had fallen to him because no one else could be trusted.

But it was also a fact, he continued, that so far the director of restaurant and hotel food had lost three warehouses to "bandits."

I wondered if we might head out to Savra. We might at

least find out if Shapallo was still in the neighbourhood. "Why wait until morning?"

"Yes, yes, why not," he agreed, his tie loose and eyes bright with raki.

Mister Gina twisted round in his seat.

"Savra?"

For the benefit of the driver he pointed a finger at the windshield and we moved on to the outskirts of town, where we felt the bump across the railway lines and pushed into the night of the countryside.

After a short distance we find the long dirt track into Savra. As soon as we pull up, a group of men appear from the shadows and we all climb out. We huddle and stamp our feet while Kadris takes charge. For some reason the conversations are conducted in whispers. There are many hands to shake, and in the dark we are passed from one group of exiles to another, and at changeovers there is more hand-shaking and incomprehensible exchanges before finally we are brought to a small house belonging to an exile.

There, the conversation continues—some of it, whenever the whim takes Kadris, is passed on.

We meet Gani Hoxha, first brought to Savra as a two-year-old in the fifties. After a life spent in dormitories, Gani had moved to this house just eighteen months previously.

His wife is introduced, a woman from Kukës whose biografi had received a devastating blow after it was learnt that her uncle was "the leader of free Albanians living in Belgium." But in recent months the uncle had turned bene-factor and the living room featured a new carpet, a television set, and a fridge.

Another woman, dumpy and with prematurely grey hair, whom I would guess to be in her early to mid-forties, smiles shyly over her coffee. She coughs up the little bit of English she knows: "I am sorry. I have no English."

The food and the raki are taking a toll. I have my mind set on bed back at the hotel, when Kadris stands up. I join him, under the impression we are about to leave. Instead, once again I am invited to shake the hand of the woman who has no English. Only this time Kadris explains, "This is Leila. She has been looking after your friend Shapallo."

"Mister Shapallo." She nods, and with two quick brush-strokes Leila describes Shapallo. She raises her hand high above her head and with her forefinger drags the nail down the centre of her forehead.

27

Leila thought it was too late to disturb Mister Shapallo. She motioned us to sit down again and I forgot all about her earlier shyness. Instead of waking Shapallo at this hour, she would try to describe his arrival in Savra.

Leila knew why Shapallo had made his way here. But by the time Shapallo arrived in Savra, the aid and medicine had come through and gone—first the Italians, then the British and the Red Cross.

It was nightfall. Nobody was up to guide a straggler off the road. In Savra there were no outside lights, and Shapallo had wandered onto the path leading to the old dormitories and fallen into a trench. In the morning he was found by children, who ran off with news of a stranger lying dead in the ditch.

By the time she got to him, Shapallo was sitting up in the trench, like a man taking a bath.

The man in the "bath" gazed back at her. She asked him where he had come from—and Shapallo had to think about this before answering, "Topojani."

The crowd peeled away, and the few remaining hands assisted Shapallo from the ditch. He could hardly stand, to support himself, and it took three of them to steer Shapallo to the doorway of the nearest abandoned dormitory.

The ceiling was low and Leila described a figure bowing his head, like a figure burrowing into a headwind.

Curiously, nothing of Shapallo's resemblance to the late and departed Emperor was mentioned. It had been the same thing at Gjaza: no comparison had been made. No one had been jolted to recognition. In Gjaza, on the other hand, there was no television or newspapers or radio, but surely a few exiles would have seen postage stamps.

Leila had simply gone to the aid of an old tramp. There was no royal swagger, such as Zog had taken with himself into exile, tipping London hotel staff with bits of gold. Nor had there been an attempt on Shapallo's part to pass himself off as a wandering prince who had found shelter among the lower orders.

Leila had seen an old man, wasting away, who curled up on the floor of the dormitory, clasping himself against the cold.

Leila and Gani left him there asleep and went around

the exiles asking for, and taking, whatever could be spared —a mattress, some blankets, clothing. Gani brought him a shaving razor, and Leila a bucket of water and some tallow to rub against his face. And when the sun dropped past its midday point and began to catch the plastic over the windows, Gani stood Shapallo up before the reflection and helped to shave him.

This is when I might have expected to learn the surprise of the Emperor's face emerging from the bearded growth. But again, nothing, and it occurred to me that Shapallo had moved beyond the age of the Emperor's final year, beyond the official age of, shall we say, "a grey vitality," to genuine old age.

Shapallo had grown to a helpless old man who had to be helped, like a child, into new clothing.

Leila brought him a tomato. But it was next to useless; Shapallo's teeth skated against its smoothness. He couldn't break the skin. So she had to chop it up and feed it to Shapallo in cubes, as if to a baby.

She heated up a cup of hot water. A few minutes later, they were all taken by surprise when Shapallo pissed his pants.

The next morning we follow Leila along the mud paths to Shapallo's dormitory. Another overcast day. But to the southeast it is clearer, and we can see the mountains there spotted with snow. This is where the wind is coming from, against which we're defenceless.

A scarf is the only measure Leila has taken against the wind and the cold. Over her shoulders the fields are a frozen sea of mud.

She has some coffee for Shapallo, and a piece of precious meat. Schnitzel, or even fowl.

I have the letter of introduction from Munz, which I haven't let go from my hand, in my pocket. Even Kadris is slightly nervous. He keeps adjusting his tie and riding the collar button over his Adam's apple, blowing on his hands and shuffling his feet.

From behind the screens dogs or some other creatures stand on their hind legs and scratch at the bamboo, and pant after our passing shadows.

Leila stops to say that, really, she would have preferred to have given Mister Shapallo some advance warning of our visit. Then she passes on something to Kadris which surprises for its protective tone. "Mister Shapallo," she says, "is an intensely private man."

We enter a small courtyard, where Leila calls out to Shapallo; and without waiting she pushes on the door. We go through.

There is a trace of recent heat; there is the faintest smell of kerosene.

A sheet of plastic flapping in the window is the only distraction from the figure sitting in bed. His knees are drawn up, a grey saddle blanket is pulled around his shoulders. And no matter how much I have prepared myself for this moment it still comes as a shock to find so abundantly alive the features from the postage stamps and the monuments, from the busts and the schoolbooks, the paintings and photographs.

Equally, the rather gruesome L-shaped scar tissue does nothing to encourage comparison. The Emperor, everyone says, had beautiful skin.

We shake hands—Shapallo not exactly wholeheartedly, and me with the charlatan's smile of a politician visiting a hospital wing.

I'm not sure where to start. Kadris, taking the matter into his own hands, begins to explain something. Then Leila pushes in and hands Shapallo his coffee. Shapallo suddenly perks up. He leans forward and Leila sits the pillows behind him.

The easiest thing would be to hand over Munz's letter and let Munz explain. Shapallo nods for me to lay the envelope on the bed beside him. It appears he is not about to give up his coffee while it is hot, and of course, two hands are required to tear open an envelope.

It is not going at all how I would have liked, how I had imagined. The seating arrangement is the immediate problem. There is nothing to anchor us to this room. We have to stand, and along with the barrenness of the room we add to its temporariness, as though what I want to know might be gleaned over a brief question-and-answer session, after which we will jump on our bikes and disappear as mysteriously as we arrived.

A short moment passes, and I wonder whether the strain of silence has become unbearable even for Shapallo, because next he hands the coffee back to Leila and tears open Munz's letter.

We watch while he reads—we follow him all the way down the winding path to the end. Then he drops the letter and looks up in amazement.

"New Zealand? New Zealand?" he asks.

Suddenly he is very excited. He is full of questions. Mainly to do with Munz. Is he here? Shapallo tries to look around us, lest Munz is about to spring through the door and surprise.

Shapallo wants to know when we can expect Munz. Is he sitting outside in a car? Will he be arriving tonight, tomorrow?

Originally Munz had intended to make the trip, but at the last moment a visiting trade delegation grounded him. Besides, he didn't think he'd be of use to Shapallo in Lushnje. He was better positioned to be of help in Tirana, if indeed it was help that Shapallo wanted.

All this is explained to Shapallo.

"Ah, Tirana." A nod of recognition.

Then I get Kadris to explain to Shapallo how I had read about him in a newspaper.

Shapallo is amused to hear this. He and Kadris weigh in on some topic. I get the feeling Shapallo has asked where New Zealand is, because I hear "Australis" mentioned, and the old man flops back against the pillows and glances at the wall with all this new and unexpected information.

It's difficult to know the best place to start. That is to say, which life to begin with. The one as the dentist, the one as Hoxha's shadow, or Shapallo's current circumstances.

Then Kadris gives me the hurry-up. "Ask what you wish to know. Mister Shapallo is waiting . . ."

So I begin on a rather lame note and ask whether he ever met Hoxha.

Once, he says, and turns back from the wall with a smile.

Nothing was said, nor was he given any advance warning.

"Like you," he says, with a friendly smile. But as he laughs, his eye catches Leila and his mood changes.

Something sharp is said, and Leila responds by gathering up the dishes. We wait until the door closes, then Kadris explains what just happened.

"Mister Shapallo did not wish Leila to know about his past. No one in Savra, he asks, must know. You say people in New Zealand know, yes? This is incredible. But in Savra, no. May I tell Mister Shapallo that you understand this, perfectly?"

"Perfect."

"But there is another problem."

He pauses there to get the rest from Shapallo, and is obviously pained by the next piece of news.

"Yes," he says very earnestly. "I am the problem, because as Mister Shapallo says, I must know everything in order for you to know. It is complicated, I think."

"Yes."

We agonise over that one for a few minutes. I'm completely lost for a quick answer.

But it is Shapallo who lets us off the hook. He coughs for our attention. He sits further up in bed. I receive a sympathetic smile before Shapallo turns his attention to Kadris.

For the next few minutes Shapallo explains himself quietly, while Kadris answers with impassioned assurances. Kadris's words, which are lifted from his heart, are met by Shapallo's sober nods. The end of the problem is signalled by a short burst of relieved laughter from Kadris.

"Mister Shapallo was very worried of me. He thought I might be *sigourimi*."

Shapallo is less than mirthful, but reassured, I think, and we resume where Shapallo left off.

"Mister Shapallo also wishes to say this happened many, many years ago. Another lifetime."

A door had opened, and in had strode a number of men. Only one he recognised—a tall man with a tanned face and excellent teeth.

The man with the excellent teeth had smiled, and that was it. The Great Leader had turned on his heel and left the room.

28

From this first encounter I take away the year in which Shapallo was yanked from his old life and fitted out with the Emperor's features.

Shapallo's abduction, curiously enough, coincides with the year of Harry Hamm's visit; on that occasion the most spectacular clue to Albania's changed relationship with the Soviet Union is an abandoned building site in downtown Tirana.

The Palace of Culture had been intended as a kind of matching colossus to the Palace of Culture in Warsaw. Khrushchev personally delivered the blueprints, and in 1960, the first spade of dirt had been turned over. Three years later Harry Hamm wrote of cranes standing in "mournful silence." Everywhere he went, he found the hotels empty.

Just one year earlier five hundred "engineers and shock brigade workers" from the Ukraine, from Moscow, from

Sverdlovsk, from the Urals, had checked into the Dajti. Now, in Tirana, and up and down the "Albanian Riviera" as well, the hotels have been abandoned by Eastern European vacationists who, the previous year, had responded in droves to the colourful posters of the Ionian Sea.

"The Cyrillic script ceases to appear in hotel registers," writes Harry Hamm. The May Day speeches criticise the Soviet deviationists' path; the eyes of the crowd listening in Skanderbeg Square scan the skies over Tirana for a reply from the giant neighbour to the north.

Fake landscapes are painted: rocket launchers and anti-aircraft guns appear on mountain slopes; armies of men, like the small plastic figures that fall out of cereal boxes in the West, stand in Albanian valleys.

Against these measures, a cardboard cutout for the esteemed leader is perhaps the least extravagant precaution. Around this time, as I recall, I first heard the voice of Tirana come from Cliff Dalziel's shed.

29

One day a man from Kukës had arrived in Topojani, out of the blue, to take Shapallo's photograph. The request of the Party, the photographer explained, and Shapallo shrugged off the inconvenience.

He mentioned the episode to his wife, how he had stood before the wall of his clinic while the photographer sheltered under a dark blanket, but then thought no more of it.

Time passes, and one day men in military uniform turn up at his clinic.

This time Shapallo has a patient with him; smiling confidently down at his patient, to eyes full of trust above a mouth stranded wide, Shapallo says he will be right back.

He washes his hands—this, from habit—and follows the men outside to a waiting jeep.

The soldiers invite him to get in the back and Shapallo obliges. Everyone is exceptionally polite. The driver comments favourably on the day. The wind is from the direction of the coast, sticky with tanning oils—momentarily the men fall silent.

Shapallo is offered a cigarette. When he declines the soldier reacts with surprise. These are the small human moments which can fill an abyss of worry. And again, when a goat stands its ground in the track, preventing the jeep's passage, all the men in the jeep laugh—even Shapallo. Soon the jeep has to cautiously chop down a gear for children playing over the track, and again Shapallo is reassured. Clearly he is among men with children of their own. Theirs is a shared perspective and he thinks no harm can possibly come to him.

Since there were no vehicles in Topojani, perhaps twice a year Shapallo would walk into Kukës. On foot it was a journey of seven or eight hours, longer if there was bad weather. Over the years he had come to know every bend, the change of sound where the river leaves the valley floor and plunges vertically into noisy, turbulent pools. There are vistas to look forward to, places to rest, and elsewhere, the long, exposed stretches without shelter from the burning sun.

Shapallo described all these places—landmarks quickly accounted for in the jeep. They pass lines of people and mules from neighbouring villages—with their "maps" of rest stops, places for toilet, places off the track to feed the mules, to rest up. And the thing that had amazed Shapallo was the way the jeep just swallowed up the passing landscape. Time condensed. There had been none of the familiar sense of entering into and departing; instead, the horizon just kept flicking over like a deck of cards, until, unbelievably as Shapallo described it, there it was, already, the end of the gorge and the sprawl of the plain.

In Kukës, while getting out of the jeep he catches a glimpse of his dentist's coat in the side mirror and he hopes aloud that this "business" will not take long. To one of the soldiers standing outside a barrack-like building, he mentions that he has a patient waiting back at the clinic. The soldier nods, but then looks away without interest.

Shapallo described the office he was shown to. There is a wooden desk, a few chairs. A room which doesn't get day-to-day use. An ashtray has not been emptied.

And there, pinned to a wall, is a line of photographs. There is no need to step closer. The photographs have been enlarged, and at first glance Shapallo passes them off as military interest in topography.

But the ridge, he discovers, is his nose. The hollows are his eyes. These are the features which stare back from his shaving mirror each day. Only they have been enlarged, apparently in an attempt to see deeper into his face, and this is the biggest shock for Shapallo, this idea of his face opened up and pored over as if it were a map belonging to someone else.

The two officers who join Shapallo a few minutes later are courtesy itself. They regret the inconvenience of it all. They wish they had been able to give prior notice, but they hope he will understand the sensitivity and the urgency surrounding this "business."

Shapallo says no, he doesn't understand. He doesn't understand any of it. He tells the officers he has a patient waiting for him back at his clinic. Furthermore, there is his family to consider. They will surely be worried. It is already late, and now, no doubt, he will have to stay overnight in Kukës.

The two officers exchange a look; one feels in his pocket for a packet of cigarettes, which he pushes across the desk.

But Shapallo isn't interested. He announces that he is leaving. That he has had enough of this intrigue. He has a patient waiting. His family . . .

He pushes his chair out noisily. He starts for the door. And now his hand is on the doorknob.

"Comrade Shapallo," says one of the officers; his voice is unhurried and calm. "Comrade Shapallo, please come here and sit down."

"It is not necessarily bad news," says the other officer.

"No?"

"No."

"Mister Shapallo," continues the first officer, "you have been chosen for a very special task."

30

We popped back to Leila's apartment, having tired Shapallo out. He said we were welcome to come back later, but by the time we reached the door his eyelids were closed.

It is colder in Leila's flat than it is outside. All the past winters have collected in its cold plaster walls, and the old kerosene heater is hopelessly outmatched.

In the doorway Leila's mother, an old woman dressed in black from head to toe, smothers Kadris in kisses and then treats me to the same enthusiasm, clasping her hands around my neck and dragging my head down to rub her face against my cheek.

The main room is oppressively crowded with pillows, blankets, eating utensils, and clothing. From this debris rises an American sweatshirt in red, white, and blue, and Leila's thirteen-year-old daughter, Beatrice, shyly says hello.

The television set is a surprise. Leila explains it is a gift from her father, Ali Starova, who also, as it emerges, is the reason for the family's exile to Savra. When Kadris asks Guria when the last time she saw her husband was, the old woman slaps a hand over her heart and howls at the ceiling. Then she scuttles off to find a photograph.

It is an old black-and-white wedding photograph of a young and strikingly good-looking woman and a slim, dark man. This is the man she married, and of whom her memories have not advanced beyond 1944. He led well on the dance floor in those days.

The other photograph she shows us is a Polaroid she received in 1982. Here is Ali some forty years later. The Polaroid had been taken in his living room at home, in New York City. Ali sits at the end of the couch, one arm draped poignantly over the vacant place beside him. On his other side—at bookshelf height—stands a small, artificial Christmas tree.

Here, surely, is a life impossible for Guria to conceive. I seem to be looking at a man familiar with popcorn and baseball on television and the subway connections to various parts of the city. It is staggering to think of this man sharing a piece of history with these two women in Savra. The man in the Polaroid gives the impression of being more than a little out of shape, but by the same token comfortable with his condition. A man resigned to fate is what I'm getting at; Guria's husband did not look like an enemy of the people.

Leila pours the coffee, then sits down beside her mother to explain the story of the man in the Polaroid.

Ali Starova had been a follower of King Zog. After liberation the Communists turned on the enemies within, and because the collaborators and Royalists were perceived to have lived under the same roof, Ali was caught in the roundup.

He spent four years in jail, in Korcë, before escaping to Yugoslavia. With Ali gone, the regime looked to see what he had left behind.

Guria spoke of the camps she and Leila had passed through. She ticked them off on her fingers—Valiasa, Carrik,

Kamez, and Pluk—her crinkly old eyes blinking at the mention of each one.

She described how she used to scavenge grain from the fields—a teaspoonful at a time.

In the late fifties she had received word from Ali. He was in France, of all places. There was just that one letter, and then a twenty-five-year silence. She assumed Ali had died, because there was no word until 1982, when she received a letter and the Polaroid of a plump man, bald, jowly, and with glasses. The television set and some money had quickly followed. But in 1986 a friend of Ali's in New York wrote to inform Guria of her husband's death. And that was her marriage.

Leila had married in Pluk, some time in the seventies. She had married another exile, the son of a man accused of waging "propaganda against the regime." Surprisingly, the son's biografi had been overlooked. Xherat had been given a "preferred job" in animal husbandry, and this oversight, so Guria had reasoned at the time, could only be good for Leila's biografi and those of future generations.

Leila had had three sons by Xherat. A few months earlier, the boys had sent their mother a photograph from Italy. In the photo, Eduart, Markelian, and Fatmir have met with a crowd of boat refugees under a fountain in Rome. Despite their new clothes, all the Albanians appear to be stunned by their new circumstances. There is an unmistakable longing, as well—and it comes of the refugees, fifteen of them, all at once drawing in their breath to stare bleakly down the tunnel of the camera lens.

I thought back to what Shapallo had said about his first

years in the block, the distress the image in his shaving mirror caused him and his desperate recall of the blown-up photographs in Kukës, this "looking-glass" and link back to his old life, to Topojani. Every moment alone he had entered the photographs and retraced an imaginative journey back up the remote mountain gorge, to his other life as a dentist, husband, and father, and each time, he said, the patient hadn't left the clinic and he was just able to resume where he had left off.

And much later, back at the hotel in Lushnje, lying on my bed and trying to ignore the stench along the corridor, I thought back to life on Kansas Street and Cliff's crude attempt to cut off his past.

A few days before I was due to fly out, I had called round to say goodbye to Cliff.

Bess had answered the door. She thought Cliffy was out and checked with a glance down the steps. But there was no light on in the basement. I had already looked. So she said, "Oh dear, you had better come in."

We sat in the living room, Bess on the edge of an armchair, carefully studying me.

"You know, I barely remember you at all," she said. "Not really. I remember your uncle and aunt. And, of course Louise . . . I am sorry for what happened. But we weren't close. People tended to feel uncomfortable around Cliffy."

"Cliff's quite a character," I said, and Bess thought about that.

"Of course, things haven't turned out the way I once thought they would." And here, she managed to laugh. "My father, he used to say to me, 'Bess, make a wish.' Well, Cliff was not that kind of man. As you know, he worked with his hands."

This was my first time in the house proper, and over the hearth I noticed a line of dark squares on the wallpaper.

Bess said, "You're looking at where our photographs used to hang. Cliff took them all down. Not that it has made any difference. They might as well be up."

She inclined her head towards a gilt-edged picture stand. There was a hole where the photograph used to be.

"Shame about that one. It was the only one we had of Cliff and his parents in Sheffield. That's in England. Cliff was once English, as you might well have been aware."

Bess said she used to like to sit in the chair where I was now.

"When the children were young, I could alternate between the green hills out the window and the black chimneys of Sheffield."

Suddenly Bess stopped and caught me off-guard, with a smile. She just wanted to say how happy she was that I had thought to visit. She was glad I had come.

"There's not the same opportunity to talk when Cliff's around," she said.

Then she put on the jug and returned with a tray.

She sat down, once again balancing on the edge of her armchair. "There is something else I would like to talk about," she said.

She gazed back at the wall, to another blank space, and prised from it another story. We went from one vacated space to another. Bess explained them all. The holiday snaps. The children's triumphs, from back-yard play to graduation,

Cliff at a ham radio operators' convention. "It's a shame you can't see for yourself. But Cliff is the short one. The tall man with the badges pinned to his hat is from Anchorage. I remember Cliffy saying he was the one in regular contact with Russian fishermen in the Kurile Islands."

From what Bess had to say, I imagined the photographs showing Cliff progressively impatient with the photo taker. Increasingly, I imagined Cliff half in and half out of photographs, wanting to take leave of the situations he is obliged to participate in, and all the time craving a different life.

Of the happier times there were photographs of Cliff and Bess with the kids at the beach—collecting agar out of the red and white seaweed tossed up on the south Wairarapa coast; a more summery one of the family lolling among the sandhills and grass at Riversdale; Cliff looking up from hammering in a tent peg; Cliff with a 1960s sun-glazed contentment, as he carries his shoes and socks across the mud flats at low tide.

I found Bess gazing at the far end of the wall, and for the life of me I could not superimpose over that abandoned square a picture of Cliff on skis. In fact, I found it difficult to believe in any of the faded blocks of wallpaper coloured in by Bess.

I wondered where the photographs were, and whether I might see them for myself. I asked Bess this, and her eyes froze.

"Don't you see? This is what I have been trying to tell you. Cliff took them all down."

"Yes, but I thought, perhaps if I could see them?"

Bess shook her head at my slowness.

"Cliff burnt them. Every single photograph that was up

there." It had happened a few weeks after his retirement.

"Cliff took down all the photographs and incinerated them."

31

"The only thing I felt then was that I was King, and born to be one. I experienced next such a delicious feeling, hard to express . . ."

It was the occasion of Shapallo's first public outing as the Emperor's understudy, and as his motorcade entered the Tirana football stadium, the crowd rose to its feet with a deafening cheer.

He was introduced to the players from both teams, and as he moved along their line the players bowed, or smiled so easily and willingly that Shapallo, out of gratitude for their easy acceptance of him in the Emperor's clothes, smiled handsomely back.

At the correct moment, and as he had been drilled to, he took a step backwards and glanced skyward to summon a dark speck in the west which grew to a squadron, and seconds later, planes swooped low and noisily over the stadium.

The conjuror's timing was excellent on this occasion, but Shapallo was mindful that he could never outdo the Emperor. It was said that during a trip to a drought-stricken area, Hoxha had raised a hand and stroked life-giving rain from the dusty air.

Timing was the essential thing here. The proof of the

pudding. In the event of an earth shudder, it would best be seen to concur with some prescient acknowledgement from the Emperor: a tilt of the head, a momentary withdrawal from conversation to reflect, a hand raised as if to summon forth, a quickly withdrawn smile—these were to be accepted as godly commands. If it had rained, then surely it was a case of the Great Leader having divined that the moment was right.

At the soccer stadium Shapallo had allowed his eye to wander, at first unwittingly animating large sections of the crowd wherever his gaze happened to pause, then more wilfully tempting first himself and then the crowd, encouraging a thousand voices to chant, "May every day be a birthday for Enver!" The noise caused even the players down on the pitch to gaze up at the terraces. A tilt of his head sent a flutter through several thousand flags.

Encouraged, Shapallo waved—and the crowd, they adored him. Shapallo said he had never before felt so loved.

Some minutes later, he shook his head, and the watchful crowd expressed for him his disappointment at a missed opportunity. Down on the field the players hung their heads.

Now the crowd was on its feet, chanting—wishing Shapallo a long and happy life. May he prosper. May the sun always single out the Great Leader with its warmth. And as he was ushered by anxious officials and minders towards the car down on the pitch, Shapallo had thought of his patients, the way they used to come to the door silent with dread—and God willing, afterwards left, shaking him by the hand. He got in the back of the limousine happily reassured in the knowledge that he had pleased.

———

Many of the questions I have for Shapallo revolve around the business of being king. How, for example, do you abandon one life which has left its marks while laying claims to having lived another? I would have thought that physical resemblance to the Great Leader would serve Shapallo well only at a distance.

These things of course had concerned Shapallo too, as he was especially mindful that his continued existence and plausibility went hand in hand.

He mentioned one of his minders, a man called Tef, who had stuck it out with him from start to finish and never failed to refer to him in any other way but "Comrade Enver." In the early days Shapallo had asked for newsreels of Enver Hoxha so he could study the Emperor's mannerisms and idiosyncrasies. He'd asked Tef for photographs that might show the Emperor on the front foot, or surprised, or magnanimous.

"And?"

We happened to be sitting on Shapallo's bed at this moment, like birds on a wire, and Shapallo reached across Kadris to tap my knee.

"Nothing," he said.

Instead, Tef had brought him books on French culture and history, and he had reminded Shapallo, "Remember, Comrade Enver, you are partial to all things French."

So he read voraciously—everything that Tef brought him. Poetry. Novels. Books on the French language. He read to fill in the time. But later his appetite grew and he started to read with increasing awareness that he had been set on a quest.

It had taken some time, years in fact, for Shapallo to

arrive at the place Tef had hinted, but one afternoon in 1970 Shapallo sat down with a new book. He was only a few chapters into *Mémoires* when he put the book down and began to pace up and down in his room, greatly agitated by his arrival in the court of the Sun King, and of course, by the knowledge that everything he needed and wanted to know was here at his fingertips.

For the next hour Shapallo reeled off the Sun King's axioms, as if they were his own.

He described Louis's vain pleasure in singing in private passages of opera prologues which were full of his praises. Even at public dinners, with his entire court present, Louis would shamelessly hum these praises between his teeth.

Louis had had a medal struck with a globe of the world balancing on the tip of his sword, and with the motto *Quad libet licet*: I can do with it what I please.

To the poet who composed the finest sonnet in praise of the King, Louis awarded a medal of himself, represented in the figure of the Sun, despatching clouds and chasing away the night birds and monsters.

Upon the gate of one of the Jesuit colleges in Paris, Louis struck out the name of Jesus, whose rule of order was set on every Jesuit-owned building, and substituted his own name instead.

Louis had depended on an extensive network of spies, the most important source being the post-office chief, since Royal Omniscience extended to weeding out the slightest complaint or contempt for the King—a throwaway phrase was often enough.

Shapallo quoted from a traveller's journal: Lord Montague, a visitor to Louis's Versailles, had counted more than two hundred pictures and statues of Louis in his house and garden. "He is strutting in every panel and galloping over one's head in every ceiling . . . and if he turns to spit he must see himself in person or as his vice regal, the Sun."

He closed with a description of a drawing Thackeray had done of Louis. The drawing, if I have understood this correctly from Kadris's sweaty translation, contained three figures. On the left, Thackeray portrayed the young King as a tailor's dummy, with a wig, false calves, and high-heel shoes. In the centre he had drawn a small bald man called "Louis"—to the right, a sketch of the combination of the tailor's dummy and the little bald man, and Thackeray captioned the drawing: "Louis, the King. The greatest actor of Royalty the world has seen!"

"When I read that," said Shapallo, "I experienced real hope. Of course, I must tell you that I had known I would have to act, like an actor, but until that moment it had never occurred to me that Enver had been doing the same."

32

One of Enver Hoxha's favourite camera hands had been Zerena's husband, Palli Kuke. One night before starting south I met him at the Hotel Tirana and Palli told me about his work.

Every camera angle had to be approved by the Press Board of the Central Committee of the Party, and this office had direct contact with Ramiz, who filled a kind of producer's role.

Only the right side of Enver was to be filmed: Palli said Enver had a problem with his right eye. "It was slightly smaller."

Specific rules determined how close Palli could go with the camera. "You could never go so close as to get only the head—the shot had always to contain the body, so his wrinkles wouldn't show."

Enver had to be presented as youthful, so Palli was obliged to use filters to soften the image.

"He was a great master at working the camera. A great actor and a director with extraordinary capacities," said Palli.

"We could tell by Nexhmije's eye if everything was perfect or not," he said.

Nexhmije always stood behind Enver, as consort, but also as wardrobe consultant and director's assistant. Nexhmije had to make sure everything was in place on the set before the show could begin.

"On this occasion we had made all the preparations in the Hoxha residence. Everything," he recalled, "was ready. The word came that Enver and Nexhmije were on their way up the street.

"You should understand," he said, "it was as if the air moved when they came into a room. The camera hands were the only ones allowed to move around, but we had to move in such a way as to prevent creating an air current.

"I was moving very slowly so as to show that I was not aware of what I was seeing or hearing. When, quite unexpectedly, Enver changed course. This was completely unscheduled. Enver did not enter the house as planned but went to sit in the park opposite. This set off a terrible confusion inside the house.

"Now, as Enver reached the park he started towards a bench. His intention was clear. He was going to sit down.

"At that moment, a huge man I had seen in the house rushed out with a pillow. He arrived just in time, and as Enver lowered himself the huge man placed the pillow, and quickly disappeared so that Enver would not feel embarrassed.

"Such things we did not film."

"Enver's death? Oh. Oh. Oh." He clasped a hand to his cheek. "Everything on television had to be about Enver. Nexhmije was director and our instructions were to show only film which would suggest a catastrophe was about to follow.

"I was with Enver to the end. Even in death. The cameraman had to be there with the body."

33

This morning the windows in Leila's apartment are misted over, and white. I can hardly move for the cold. The session with Shapallo last night straggled on into the small hours. Shapallo lost his shyness around Leila and she joined us and upheld a polite but formal interest, to begin with. But as the evening wore on, she corrected Kadris's dates and told her own stories. We had a bottle of raki to warm our insides and soon we were laughing and conversing easily. At some point Guria appeared at the door to say she had found some bedding. And after that, we were better able to relax, without any further thought to the walk ahead of us, back to Lushnje.

I don't know what hour it was when we bade Shapallo farewell. Leila had already retired. Our last view of Shapallo was from the window, of the old man crouched over his Bunsen burner, warming his hands, his greatcoat hanging from his shoulders, looking less like an emperor than a shag lifting its wings, ready for flight.

There's some rustling coming from the other side of the wall. It's the mystery room between Leila's door and the communal toilet. Donatella, Fatmir's eighteen-month-old daughter, is up. I hear her shrieks and wide-eyed voice and Guria's purring from the other room.

I wear everything to bed. All I take off are my boots. Kadris has the couch on the other side of the room. He falls asleep with his tie still knotted. A corpse in a suit buried beneath Leila's and Guria's black coats.

A horse coughs in the fields, and then it is quiet again.

I get up at first light and wander outside. A line of women scarved up against the cold shoulder their picks and shovels out to the fields. Stumbling after them is a man in blue trousers and a blue jacket. He has just spotted me and can't believe his eyes.

I wave, and he turns after the women.

The faint beginnings of a sun draw the cold up from the earth; it rises through the thick soles of my Dolomites. These same conditions are all but ignored by a girl of about fourteen walking by in a cotton shirt. Her hard young breasts point ahead and she trails a head of dirty hair on her shoulders. She's carrying a prize in her hand—a piece of bread sprinkled with sugar, a far cry from when the murals on the walls of the bread and fruit shops were hidden by piles of food, and children threw grapes in the air, like peanuts.

During his years in the block Shapallo had not wanted for anything. The times when the Emperor was unwell Shapallo was obliged to skip a meal so that, together, Hoxha and he might grow wan and stingy-mouthed at the thought of food. Otherwise, as in a child's world, everything was provided for.

As in a child's world he did as told—for instance, he must fix his eye on an imaginary face at the very edge of the crowd. On the rare occasion of a crowded room he must resist the entrapment of detail and instead focus on doorways and distant walls.

These instructions had come from Tef, the smiling official, who gave Shapallo every encouragement to think of himself as Emperor.

On his arrival in the block, Shapallo was given a dressing gown. He was also given Chinese underclothing. A pair of sandals for indoor wear. A cap like Enver's. Several double-breasted suits of grey flannel, and that was it. Clothes for public occasions. Otherwise in private he lived in a dressing gown and sandals to prevent another identity from emerging through a second change of clothing.

He had been in the block three months, and this particular day, which was the Emperor's birthday, Tef showed up with flowers, sweet Williams, for Shapallo.

Weeks, months passed by, and the official provided Shapallo with other little surprises. Sometimes he turned up with chocolate. Or ice cream. Enver liked chocolate and ice cream. At other times there were books by Enver's favourite authors—Jerome K. Jerome, Jack London, Shakespeare, and Dickens. Dickens especially. But more often he brought Shapallo chocolate, Turkish delight, and sometimes confectionary from abroad, wrapped in bright-coloured crepe paper and bows.

"I have no family," he told Shapallo one time, smiling with embarrassment.

In 1970, Tef arrived with a television set, and together, like a couple of aging boardinghouse indigents, they sat downstairs to watch the New Year music show. Every so often, as Shapallo recalled, the camera would leave the musicians and singers onstage and search among the audience for Enver's straight back and ready smile. And whenever this happened, Tef would chuckle and push the chocolates in Shapallo's direction.

A young woman was singing. She wore her hair long, gypsy-like, and bell-bottom jeans and a halter neck which left her stomach bare. This was extremely risqué. She was singing a love song, and when the cameras moved up close to her face, Shapallo said, he saw the grown-up features of his oldest daughter, Vata; the same pear-shaped cheeks, he said, the big brown eyes which had so often stood by the door to his clinic, watching him, quiet as a shadow, sometimes for as long as half an hour before he would look up with a start and notice her.

He began to call to the woman on television, calling out his daughter's name.

At that moment the cameras returned to mingle in the audience. Shapallo breathed out and sat back in his chair, and as he did so, he noticed that Tef had been watching him with concern, his face drawing to a professional judgement.

Shapallo had felt reasonably sure that for all his generosity and his gifts, Tef was still an official who made out reports, just as he was confident there were others, whose faces he never saw, with an interest in his "progress."

On this occasion Shapallo nodded silently, and the danger passed.

Last night he explained that his daughters were eight and ten when he was abducted. He volunteered this information—tapping the side of his head to add: "But in here they continued to grow to adulthood, to marry and have children."

In absentia, Shapallo had continued to celebrate their birthdays, construct conversations, even arguments. In this world he continued to have family responsibilities. He worried after them. At one time he had even considered, that is to say he had imagined, plans for their leaving Albania.

There had been few opportunities for Shapallo to notice the drift of the country outside the block. His visits were too short for him to form an impression. But he had noticed slight but quite palpable changes in the crowd. The devotion of the earlier years had dissipated. There was still a sea of flags, but these were now held in hands which had lost all feeling.

He started to notice the general neglect. The buildings needed painting. It seemed that everything outside the block had gone into a slouch, as though the stitching that ran throughout the city had started to unravel. He overheard the gardener complain to the soldiers that there was no meat, and the soldiers complain back that machinery lay idle for want of parts.

Shapallo seemed to think it had been around the early eighties that a radical change was introduced into his diet. Meat and fish were virtually eliminated, and a monotony of soups was forced upon him.

The Emperor was dying and, accordingly, a sort of cheerful emaciation was expected of Shapallo. Already, at Tef's insistence, Shapallo relied on a walking stick. On the same advice, these days he allowed himself to be bodily assisted to the rostrum, to take in a parade. He was to smile at the silliness of all the fuss and give every indication that recovery lay just around the corner.

But on television, Shapallo noticed, the Emperor moved slowly and painfully. No longer did the cameras lovingly soak up the detail of Enver's favoured side, but caught him at oblique angles before flitting off elsewhere.

One night there appeared a stooped and frail old man standing on a beach. In one hand Enver held an orange; his other hand pointed to the horizon, to where the cameras obediently sought out the "true boundary between suffering and dignity."

Towards the end, less was asked of Shapallo. The organised mass rallies were fewer. Increasingly the Emperor's appearances were for a television audience: footage of his walking through a sunny olive grove, of his standing between two farmworkers, like a gold medallist, or in a classroom, sitting snuggled up to a litter of infants dressed in blue smocks.

It was around this time that Shapallo started to construct plans to send his family abroad. He toyed with the idea of a wealthy uncle in Italy, but there were unforeseen problems with that scenario. A wealthy uncle on its own was a fairly distant proposition, but Italy, as a place, its smells, its quality of light, its tastes, was unfathomable. There was nothing for Shapallo imaginatively to latch on to, and so in the end he could not bear to send his family away to a world which he couldn't begin to imagine and, therefore, was effectively barred from entering.

34

This morning I invited Leila to the Blerimi. Mentor was due to arrive from Tirana, and I had thought about driving into town for lunch with Leila and her mother. Kadris explained the plan, and Leila, with vague intention, picked up a hairbrush. Thoughtfully she held out a grey strand of hair; then she let it go.

"What is this Blerimi?" she asked.

Kadris described the restaurant above Lushnje with the views of the Myzeqe, and he made as if to kiss the grease of hot schnitzel off his fingertips. But he might as well have been explaining plans for Leila to visit her father's grave in New York. The hairbrush was put aside and she said she could not go to this restaurant, because she had never been to a restaurant. She didn't know what to expect—she did not like surprises. There was no persuading her, and Guria went along with Leila's decision.

If the Blerimi lay outside the boundaries of every-day experience, then Savra, equally, had caught Kadris unawares—he seemed affected by the stories he had heard.

We waited another hour and decided to set out on foot for the market in Lushnje to stock up.

It was another cold day, but tolerable in the absence of any brutal wind blowing over frozen fields. Leila walked between me and Kadris; she held her shopping basket out in front as though loitering down a supermarket aisle. The previous March, she said, this same bare road had been thick with people, among them her three sons.

She spoke of the fantastic rumours which had buzzed about Savra on the day of the exodus, and how on Tirana Television they had learnt of a "small number of hooligans" commandeering a number of ships in Durrës.

"Then Eduart had tuned in to RAI and the Italians were saying something very different," she said.

The Italians had spoken of thousands clambering aboard ships.

"Thousands! They did not mention 'hooligans.' "

She asked me to tell her about Italy. The letters she had received so far were spare of detail. She wished to know more. She listened attentively. And of course, she asked me the question which Bill had told me is asked every foreigner: "How poor are we?" Television. She wanted to know how many channels there were in Italy. She had heard it said that in America people watched television in the toilet. Could I please confirm this?

I thought back to the living-room scene we had left in Savra with Guria, Donatella, and her mother, Hava, watching *Bonanza* off a Yugoslav channel. Lorne Greene was speaking English, but the subtitles had been in Serb.

In Rome I had looked up Franco Leonardi, the television writer for Il *Messaggero*, who was in no doubt of television's role in the boat exodus. He believed that a powerful transmitter built in Puglia to relay the signal to southern Italy had had the unexpected benefit of strengthening reception across the Adriatic. In the cluttered Old World offices of Il Messaggero Franco described how Albania had at last seen the truth about the outside world.

The twin realities were starkly obvious: Since the regime had given up on jamming reception, an exile seated in a cold room in Savra could watch commercials about Lancias, ankle-deep carpet, and beautiful women lowering themselves into sunken baths foaming with bubbles. If they looked up from the set, out the window, they saw mud and no prospects.

Eventually the white pebbles at the bottom of the hill ranges grew to the size of apartment boxes. Soon after, we were stepping over the railway lines and onto the main road through Lushnje.

We stopped by the hotel. I spared a thought for my things in my room upstairs. But I could not bear to go up there and touch base, even briefly.

The woman crouched inside the small candlelit cubicle thought Mentor was down at the railway station.

"A mechanical problem," said Kadris.

In Lushnje there are two markets. There is the one in the square beneath the Democratic Party Headquarters. The other is by the railway station, a sprawling area of dust and trucks.

Canvas awnings are unhooked at the back of trucks, and

out climb cold, weather-bitten travellers who have journeyed in from surrounding villages.

The men leap down casually, limber as gymnasts, eager to put arrival behind themselves and blend in. The women, with huge bags and encumbered with babies swaddled in blankets, are left to struggle out on their own; on one foot they balance, dangling their free foot below for the step, while their husbands gaze off in another direction or else cup their hands to get their cigarettes lit.

Eventually we spot the Volvo, its rear axle propped up on top of a pile of stones and Mentor, trustingly, stretched out underneath to tie on the exhaust pipe.

Kadris addresses Mentor's feet—they give a small kick, and in a jiff Mentor has wriggled out. The sight of us is the cause of great distress or sublime pleasure, I'm not sure which. He buries his face in Kadris's chest and gives a heart-rending apology for our having had to walk from Savra, but some tragedy had befallen his car in the night.

He had started out with the relatively minor inconvenience of a puncture, but had made things worse by driving on it from the hotel to the garage here. The Volvo, lopsided and with a battered wheel rim, seemed to indicate the fate of every toy that had been sent home from Italy.

The man in the garage rolled out the wheel rim. He'd made a pretty good job of hammering it back into shape. It just remained for his son to return with a bike tube from home. Bicycle tubes were the country's sole remaining source of rubber.

We were there another hour before the garageman's son showed up. In that time a truck which had driven up from the Greek border arrived with brandy, cigarettes, pasta, kerosene, goat meat, chocolate, girlie calendars, and television sets.

I bought some brandy, some meat and rice, and half a dozen bottles of kerosene.

After Mentor fitted on the wheel there followed a strange Byzantine quest for tomatoes and onions. Mentor was particularly aggressive in this pursuit. In the lowering gloom of the afternoon we drove to different parts of Lushnje, from one house to another, and in due course we found ourselves on the road headed south to Berat.

In a short while we left the road and followed a farm track for a time, until it ended in a lean-to cobbled together from loose rocks. We stayed in the car, our shoulders jammed together for warmth, while Mentor in his city shoes marched belligerently around the back of the dwelling, yelling out for the occupant. When he returned to the car he stuck a package under Kadris's nose.

It smelt like cat piss, but Kadris dreamily inhaled.

"I have not had goat cheese for many, many months," he said.

Later, back in Savra, in Leila's flat, the goat cheese was consumed in the kind of ritual silence that marks the end of a famine. Shapallo ate noisily, sucking and nibbling at the crumbling cheese between his forefinger and thumb. He sucked the cheese off his fingertips and turned his attention to the brandy, while Mentor told us a story about a priest who had been ordered by the Party to stand before his congregation and renounce his faith.

The wily old priest did as the Party asked, and addressed

the congregation, but he ended his retraction saying, "Listen very carefully. From now on, you must do as I do."

"That night," said Mentor, "the priest escaped."

We all laugh, except for Shapallo. I can see him turning it over in his head. The priest escapes. Yes. The priest escapes . . . where?

"He escapes," said Mentor simply.

35

Shapallo had been instructed on the protocol should he be cut down by an assassin's bullet. And he had been instructed to keep in mind that he should make light of his injuries while he lay in public view, since the real Emperor would survive. In the messy event of a car bomb, then all that went out the window.

It is easy to imagine a life spent behind walls in the block obsessively plotting, yearning for the Emperor's death. But curiously, by his own admission, Shapallo had hardly given it any thought. His teeth bit and he cast a thin look as if this was the wildest idea.

"Remember," he said, "I was the one who was supposed to die."

The night Hoxha died, Shapallo was awakened by an intruder. A hand shoved rudely against his mouth. There was the click of a torch.

Shapallo paused, and briefly looked up from his account. It was Tef, he said.

"I knew Hoxha was dead, or something terrible like that," he said.

And a moment later it was confirmed that something calamitous had indeed occurred, when Tef for the first time abandoned his official distance.

"My dear old friend," Tef started.

There was so little time. There he was, about to be cast back out to the real world, and yet absurdly, Shapallo suddenly felt consumed with worry over small, insignificant details.

Tef had thought to bring with him a package of clothes. But Shapallo found the trousers too short in the leg. He fussed about. He was disappointed in the colour of the shirt Tef had chosen. It was an army officer's shirt and Shapallo didn't like the flaps over the pockets.

He was given money. A map. And finally, the official offered his real name.

"Your family," he started. But when he didn't add anything, Shapallo guessed.

"Dead?"

The official nodded.

"My girls?"

"Dear Shapallo. A month after you came here."

An hour later they slipped from the house. The door from the garden creaked open and the official pushed him out to the street. Numb with grief, and like an aging Rip van Winkle, Shapallo groped through the block without a clue in which direction his best hope lay.

The Topojani of his imagination, which had sustained him all these years, was gone. His daughters' marriages, and the grandchildren he had gained—all that had been stripped away. He mourned the loss of a world, as much as he grieved for his family.

It was very late, but there were lights on in many of the villas in the block. In one window, the sight of a woman pressing her hands to her face reminded him of his own grief, and in his hour of release he found himself weeping for his children.

Tef had warned him to look out for soldiers and police, but Shapallo said he walked without a care. He felt that he couldn't be hurt any further; he had lost the capacity to fear. Soon the ground turned rough. The city sank deeper into night, and he realised that he had left the block behind. But already, after the years of captivity, he found himself out of breath, and he felt the new rawness of blisters forming over his heels and ankles.

That first night of "freedom" Shapallo had crawled into a bomb shelter in a children's playground. He described the shelter overgrown with weeds, the soggy darkness and its stink of old urine. It was damp underfoot, and without a satisfactory place to lie down he simply leant against a wall and dozed off.

He woke on the ground covered in slime and with one side of his clothing wet through. From the world above, he could hear the rusted seesaws groaning and the children's squealing and the pitter-patter of tiny feet. Hours later, a shaft of light made it to the top steps of the bomb shelter entrance. Shapallo waited until he could no longer hear children's voices, and when all was quiet he went and sat on the step farthest from the entrance and dried himself in the sun.

He waited until sundown before leaving the bunker. On the outskirts of the city a roadblock forced him off the road.

He slipped through the courtyard of a housing block. In the dark he upset a number of oil bottle crates and he ran with fright from the noise, down a short slope, and sank ankle deep into the fields.

Under these circumstances Shapallo hadn't found much use for the map. The dark bulk of a mountain stood out against the lighter skyline and he started in its direction. For hours he walked away from the city. And when he could not take another step he sat down in a field and smelt soybeans and alfalfa. He smelt the countryside and breathed in its vastness. For the first time since leaving the block he "listened" to his hunger, and while lying on his back he reached out and stuffed alfalfa into his mouth, like a farm animal.

36

On my fourth day in Savra, I was surprised to find the brigadier sitting up at Leila's table, with a coffee. I recognised him immediately as the same man I had seen stumbling through the ground mist the other morning.

He was a shy man in his late thirties. He had a round face with thin black hair which lay lifelessly to one side. A sparse stubble covered his chin. I could find nothing in his appearance that suggested privilege.

But it was a surprise, all the same, to find him under the same roof as an exile.

"We are all friends," Paitim said, and glanced away nervously.

Leila certainly thought about it. She looked up as if she had espied something very delicately balanced in the distance about to fall—and she let it go.

She got up from the table; the brigadier held out his cup and Leila silently refilled it.

The brigadier blushed and smiled, as if to say, "You see?"

He explained to Kadris how he had helped Leila in the past, pleading with and finally bribing officials to allow Leila's two eldest, Fatmir and Eduart, to attend middle school. Both times it had cost Leila three months' wages from working in the fields. This morning Paitim was visiting Leila for news from her boys in Italy.

His youngest brother, Eloni, had fled to Italy on the same ship that had taken Leila's sons, the children of exiles.

Later in the day, at Paitim's invitation, we got to meet the retired brigadier.

Despite Paitim's assurances that Leila would direct us to his family's apartment, Leila wasn't sure where the brigadier's family lived. Only seventy metres of rough ground separated the brigadier's building from the exiles' living quarters. Leila knew the building. She pointed it out but laughed at the suggestion that she come with us.

She waved us on, and turned back.

Paitim, who met us at his family's door three floors up, was at a loss to explain Leila's shyness.

"We burn under the same sun and shiver when it is cold. We experience the same crowded conditions."

All of what he said was true. The old brigadier had two of his son's wives and their children living with him, so that he and his wife had to sleep in the kitchen at night. Nevertheless, there was a feeling of space and outlook in the brigadier's family quarters. The outstanding difference that immediately took my eye were the works of Enver Hoxha, which lined a shelf, as they had the one above Cliff's bed in Kansas.

I had heard mixed reports of the old brigadier, ranging from "fair" to "prickly." One time Gani Hoxha's wife had demanded to know why the exiles weren't being paid as much as the other workers, and the brigadier had remonstrated, "What! Do you want the Americans and the imperialists to march through here next?"

He was a small, neat man seated in a cross-legged yoga position on the couch. He stared out the window to the mountains in the south, dappled with snow, meditating on the points raised by his wife.

She was angry about the exiles "having everything." By everything, she meant other possibilities. Links with the outside world.

"Their relatives abroad send them things. We have nobody abroad, therefore," she said conclusively, "we have nothing."

Paitim added that his father had been a "distinguished brigadier," always at pains not to favour the farmworkers over the exiles.

The old brigadier accepted this tribute quietly. We were having a hard time of it prising him from his interest in Trebeshina, the mountain range in the window. His wife,

Baria, had been brought up in a village lost in the long mountainous folds which were dipping into shadow.

I wondered if he could imagine himself visiting Italy, now that his son Eloni was there, and the old brigadier suddenly came alive.

"Never! I am too old to go anywhere."

"My father does not wish to go to Italy," Paitim said.

"Italy!" said the old woman, rolling her eyes and weaving a spell with her hands.

There was one place, however, that the brigadier dearly wished to visit.

"Yes?"

"Vlorë."

At the mention of Vlorë, Baria came and stood by the brigadier's side and held his hand.

The brigadier explained, "I would like very much to go back to Vlorë so I might imagine how everything was when I was a young officer."

Along with five thousand other decommissioned officers in the early fifties, and without a job to turn to, he had "answered the call of the State to drain the swamp at Savra." When the brigadier arrived here, there was one dwelling filled with prisoners from Albania's border skirmishes with Greece. The Greeks were the first to drag boulders out of the swamp, and in quick succession wave after wave of exiles had arrived, until the population of Savra had ballooned to three thousand.

We had come to the end of the coffee and raki and Turkish delight when the old brigadier unfolded his legs and spoke at length with Kadris.

"The brigadier asks if you intend to return to Italy."

"Yes," I said, which clearly was the answer he had hoped to hear. The brigadier slapped his knee. He conferred with Baria, then he passed his request on to Kadris.

"The brigadier asks that you will take a letter to his son. I believe, too, he asks that you write him as to what you see. He does not believe Eloni's reports."

Later, in the evening, Leila approached me with Kadris sheepishly in tow.

"I told Leila about your plan to visit the brigadier's son in Italy. She asks that you do the same for her sons."

Guria, hovering nearby, immediately snatched a sheet of paper from my notebook and began to scribble a note to her three grandchildren. She dashed it off with an angry kind of flourish. Whereas Paitim had sat down and, red-faced with concentration, had written, "My dearest Eloni . . ."

On this, my last night in Savra, I finally "meet" Leila's husband. It was a chance thing. I was out on the landing when the door alongside the bathroom opened, giving me a start. I was so used to it being closed that I'd come to think of it as an extension of the wall. Briefly we stared at each other before the stranger wordlessly retreated, pulling the door shut.

Whenever I had asked after Xherat I had got back an evasive answer. Sometimes Leila would flutter her fingers and make a *pffiff* sound, as if Xherat had dissolved into thin air. Or else she would parry the question and bluster: "We are a family of women!" And Guria would then unwittingly bolster the smokescreen by testifying to her daughter's strength with remarks such as "She was born with a pickaxe across her shoulder." Until we moved right off the trail with Kadris, also, chipping in, "You know, Leila is a very strong woman."

But this evening, when I ask Leila about the stranger out on the landing, she says it is her husband. She makes some general announcement which sends Guria into a high-spirited cackle. Leila blushes as Kadris mischievously shares with me what I wasn't supposed to hear. "Leila wonders why you must know everything."

In the mid-seventies, Petrit Dume, a distant relative of Leila's, was accused of being accomplice to a failed coup d'état. Dume's biografi was thoroughly examined and this investigation reverberated down various bloodlines.

The "preferred job" in animal husbandry which had made Xherat such a good catch for Leila in the first place was taken from him and he was sent to work out in the fields. The sigourimi, eager for more damning evidence against the "accomplice" to the failed coup, took Xherat and Leila in for questioning.

They questioned the two separately. Eventually the sigourimi surprised Leila by repeating things back to her which had passed strictly between her and Xherat. Of course she denied ever saying these things about the relative. But she worried nonetheless as to how the sigourimi had come to know the things they put to her.

Leila didn't budge from her position; the interrogations were stepped up. The sigourimi wanted her "evidence." They wanted her to repeat the things she had allegedly already said about Dume. They were determined that she be their second witness.

Finally, with their patience at an end, the *sigourimi* played their trump card.

They interrogated Leila and Xherat together. This time, when Leila refused to comply, the *sigourimi* walked to the window and turned their backs, and Xherat said to her, "Why don't you just admit to the things you have said to me?"

For a moment she was stunned. It was also the moment, Leila said, when she decided to divorce her husband.

Weeks passed, months, and the story emerged that Xherat had been promised his old job back in animal husbandry if he would provide the *sigourimi* with additional information against Leila's relatives.

"I could not believe that my husband would do such a thing." She recalled from a "romanciful" book she had read many years earlier how the hair of a jilted lover had turned white overnight.

"At the time I read this I did not believe it possible. But this same thing happened to me."

For thirteen years Leila had refused to speak to or acknowledge the man who lived behind the door next to the bathroom. There was no other place for Xherat to go.

In the morning Leila stood on the landing to wave goodbye. Stooped in the doorway behind her were Guria and Beatrice, with little Donatella trying to squeeze through their legs. To their right was the door to Xherat's room. That closed door in Savra, I think, signalled the worse kind of exile.

37

The distance from Savra to Vlorë, the place of the retired brigadier's youth, is no more than seventy kilometres. Enver and Nexhmije used to have a holiday house there. It was from Vlorë that Enver had hurried back to Tirana in a panic after delegates to the 1958 Tirana Congress were encouraged to speak openly, and some, to Enver's horror, had done exactly that. Vlorë was also one of the landing places during the Italian invasion. Another more compelling reason to go to Vlorë is its location on the coast. The Albanian Riviera starts at Vlorë, and on Cliff's map the road immediately climbs over the imposing Coraun mountain range to spill down the other side to ocean. This is the road on which Shapallo's surgeon and hairdresser had met their end, and the same road to which, many years later, Shapallo turned to seek anonymity.

Shapallo has come along with us. We asked him last night, and before Kadris had finished explaining that we would be gone two days, Shapallo bounced up from his bed and grabbed his coat. Then the old man wondered what the delay was about. Tonight. Tomorrow. It made no difference to him.

As we pass the turnoff to Gjaza I look to see if it registers with Shapallo. Nothing. He doesn't turn his head a whisker.

Half an hour later we enter Fier, where a large crowd is mobbing a bakery door. People are hoisted up on shoulders to reach through the iron bars of the bakery window. Kadris said there had been something on television last night about there being less than six days' supply of flour left in the country.

Further on in town, concrete bunkers compete with free enterprise stalls for the best vantage points in the market-place. There is more food in Fier than I have seen in a while. Unsuspecting ducks are cycled home. Hand-held turkeys dangle upside down. The flightier chickens are tied to bike carriers.

The main street is lined with phoenix palms. A small park is filled with pines. Then we're back to the continuum of drab concrete housing blocks. Where they end, the concrete bunkers resume. Then they too come to an abrupt halt, like flora unable to flourish because of a sudden change in soil conditions. A few kilometres on and the bunkers return, thickening up near a massive fertiliser works.

From Leven, a state farm, the road narrows to a tooth-pick and it's a straight run to the coast. We pass by acres of rusted tunnel housing. Glasshouses lie smashed. There is no wind, not so much as a breeze to disturb the dead flaps of plastic.

From his recollection, Shapallo says the area was "once wonderful eating."

On Cliff's map the area we are passing through is Apol-lonia, represented by a rich green landscape, which in the millennium before Christ formed a gateway to the Balkan highlands and Macedonia.

Nearer to Vlorë the road twists through a small range of

hills. The hillsides, terraced with olive trees, lie abandoned. A weedy undergrowth is reaching up to the lower branches, and on many of the trees the olives remain uncollected.

On Cliff's map Vlorë has been allocated a sun umbrella and it's easy to see why. The town is cupped by hills thick with olives. Even the crude housing blocks have less impact here. The relief is open-ended, because here, at last, is the sea. Small waves gallop up to a long, thin strip of tree-lined beach. Presumably in summer umbrellas get a chance to flourish in between the concrete bunkers built at regular intervals along the beach and as far as the eye can see.

The startling thing is I don't recall having seen anyone as we passed through Vlorë. In town we did a quick tour of the old statue sites. Everything had been torn down and we didn't come across another soul. Kadris said everyone was at home eating lunch. Then, after further consideration, he thought the rest may have gone abroad, to Italy.

Where the road begins to hug the beach it is possible to glance up the hill, to where the treetops fall short of concealing a remnant of Albania's architectural past. The tiled rooftop of Enver's summer house can just be seen.

The road climbs to a promontory, and on its furthest point, fenced off from the road, is the former grand residence of Hynsi Kapo, one of the few trusted friends of Enver's who was allowed to share in power. At the time of his death he had risen to become the Second Secretary of the Politburo. He is remembered mostly for his having gone to a natural death.

Surviving that memory is his three-storey clifftop residence which would not disgrace itself on the French Riviera.

But here, because of its solitariness and on the heels of the Soviet housing models, it is all the more extraordinary.

Succeeding it a few kilometres on is a modestly sized memorial to "Albania's Youth," whose devotion to the three disciplines—the military, education, and "voluntary work" —was responsible for carving the terraces on the steep hillsides.

A short distance on, Kadris points out where the students lost their lives.

We have left the coast for a valley with the ancient name of Orikum. It is lush at the entrance and snowcapped at its head. In between are the most beautiful streaks of purples and greys, soft and unworldly, like the colours found in rainbows. Here and there, the odd stone cottage, but no people and few signs of domesticity. A goat chewing its cud looks up at our passing.

Where the road begins to climb, the valley walls close up, and on the far slopes, which are sheer vertical drops, bits of terracing cling in patches; elsewhere, the terraces have subsided, dropped away as if over a waterfall, some with uprooted young trees sticking out from the spill. The older, dead ones look like bony hands.

The first vehicle of the day, an old Chinese truck, appears around the bend up ahead. A green cab belching chocolate-coloured smoke that swirls away to a kite tail. The passengers stand on the back, each person's hand resting on the shoulder of the one in front. They have come down from the pass and their heads are wrapped in see-through plastic.

Balancing on the very top of the Llogara Pass is a patch of pale blue sky. We wind down the windows and the wind feels clean. For the moment it feels as though we have left Albania. We are down to a crawl—Mentor as usual persevering with too high a gear—when Shapallo rests a hand on Mentor's shoulder, and this downward pressure slowly brings the car to a halt.

The Volvo is breathing heavily—a hissing from the radiator. Otherwise it is incredibly still. We look for eagles.

Soon we climb out. Shapallo withdraws to the side of the road with his hands clasped behind his back.

A whisper in my ear from Kadris: "Mister Shapallo wishes to have lunch now."

Leila has prepared some balls of spicy rice. They come wrapped in pages from her library of Enver's works. One page is headed "Decoding the Chinese." Another, "Meetings with Stalin."

Enver raises Mao's complaint that he had felt "like a schoolboy" in Stalin's presence, whereas he had felt himself treated to a great man's humility. He talks of their sharing a meal together. Stalin sends away the help and the two men serve each other. Later, Stalin is at pains to show Enver the toilet. In the garden, on a walk, he worries over the younger man's dress, whether he is warm enough. The page ends there, stained with rice.

Shapallo is squinting across the valley floor. What I had mistakenly thought of as a landslide of rocks, he tells me, is in fact a village twinkling in the sun.

Now of course I can see—the layering of rocks and the breathing spaces in between.

Shapallo says he visited the village about ten years ago. He can't recall its name—and on Cliff's map it doesn't even exist. It was during one of the Emperor's illnesses and Shapallo had travelled through the night to open a school in the village. The villagers threw wild roses in his path, and Shapallo recalled his trailing sooty red- and burgundy-coloured petals after the colours of the national flag. And later, when it came time to leave, he was amazed to find the villagers digging holes to plant rose shrubs over the ground which had received his footsteps.

Several years later he returned to the village. This was after the Emperor's death and Shapallo had grown a short beard to cover Enver's "genial chin." He leant on a walking stick and covered his head with a highlander's bright neckerchief. He was given itinerant's work and paid with food to collect firewood.

He spent several happy months in the village. There were no newspapers, no television, and no radios, and without such reminders Enver's profile had faded from memory faster here than in the cities. He might have stayed longer, but it was already October and he feared a winter in the lee of a mountain might finish him off.

Shapallo had seen off October before he managed to hitch a ride on a horse-drawn cart over the Llogara Pass. A farmer was headed to Dhermi to find a suitable husband for his oldest daughter. It took them all day to reach the pass, and there they found the waterfall frozen solid. It was so cold that the reins fell from the man's grasp; the horses came to a stop, and Shapallo, along with the driver, climbed down and walked back down the road to bury their hands in warm horse shit.

"But not the bride. No. No," said Kadris.

Another twenty minutes and we're at the pass. It is as Shapallo has already described, but with an interesting improvisation. A deer sculpted out of stone is attempting to lick water from a frozen waterfall.

Near the deer, a colourful stone mosaic of peasants and partisans proclaims solidarity: "In this place, September 1944, the partisans and peasants under the leadership of Hynsi Kapo fought the Germans and disarmed the Italian Fascist unit . . ."

Just over the rise, small hunting lodges in a cluster of reds and bright yellows are tucked away in a copse of pine.

Here the road is in shadow and Mentor takes it carefully, like a skater his first time upon ice. He is not liking it. The conditions have at last borne out his worst expectations. This morning he tried to persuade me with his visions of ice and snow to take the inland route. The thinner ice is cracking under the weight of the car and we have all fallen rather quiet.

But then we leave the trees and shadows behind, and the tyres begin to grip the road. Around the next bend we come face-on with the breathtaking surprise of the Ionian Sea. After the muddy Adriatic, it is vast and blue and, above all, civilising. The car slows to a halt; even Mentor is moved to gaze, for there is this wonderful sense of threshold, of our moving on to better things.

After punching into dark, icy hollows on the way up the other side, the downward journey takes us through wide-open space and sunshine. The road gleefully races out to the bend, and here the sea glances up at a surprising angle and lists away, back and forth, as we loop the stony mountainside.

Shapallo recalls that when he made this same journey several years back, the air had grown warmer at every bend, until halfway down the mountain the bride complained of the smell of horse dung on her father's hands.

On one of the bends is a military post—all window and lens trained on the horizon; we squirrel by unnoticed, zig-zagging all the way down to the bottom of the mountain.

The road briefly sinks beneath some trees, then we cross a small stream into Dhermi.

Virtually without warning the road disappears out from under us. What remains is barely wide enough for the Volvo. We push along a track which twists around the back of weathered stone dwellings and underneath patios dripping yellow, withered vines. Some of the windows have been shuttered up. The windows of a café are boarded over, its doors plastered with Democrat slogans. The only sign of life is an elderly man with a thick white moustache and wearing a Muslim skullcap.

We draw alongside so Kadris can ask where everyone has disappeared to.

"Greece!"

The man waves his hand in the direction of the coast. Then he repeats himself: "Greece!" He has a cross look, as if he has lost a bad-tempered argument.

We pick a lane down to the beach, where we find the second inhabitant, a middle-aged man neatly turned out in an officer's uniform, his shiny black boots crunching along the beach. In lovely white sunbather's sand a line of concrete bunkers sits about twenty metres above the high-tide mark.

The only other signs of trespass are a military installation and a block of worker holiday flats at the far end of the beach. The military installation stares blankly out to sea, whereas, as if to curb any longing for foreign places, the view from the workers' flats has been turned away from the horizon to behold the coastline farther south. The view is thus contorted, like a man perpetually twisted in order to stare into his own armpit.

Although Sarandë is no more than another eighty kilometres down the coast, we spend the rest of the day getting there. It all starts coming back to Shapallo, his various encampments and shelters. We stop by some other deserted worker holiday flats. The windows have been smashed, the walls blackened from campfires. Itinerants, gypsies, migrants destined for Greece have all passed through here.

Shapallo says he once spent a year living in another abandoned block of flats with a family of hickory workers, highlanders, he said, who had travelled to the coast to make a living out of crafting pipes. Sometime later we pass a family combing the roadside brush and Shapallo points out the load of hickory on their backs. One very old woman who has been spared a load is bent over nearly double from a lifetime of mule work. As late as Zog's reign women along with livestock were fair game among cattle thieves.

PARTI ENVER has been scratched on a hillside a little north of Borsh, and in the nearby deserted town itself, LIRI (freedom) has been painted over the door to a café.

We pass through the abandoned orange and olive groves. In one place we stop and help Mentor load his boot with oranges.

"Everyone has gone to Greece," says Kadris. "No time to pick or eat."

One village after another, we enter the peculiarly still air and crawl past the locked-up houses. The remains of a goat, a thin carcass, its eyes pecked out, are still chained to a feeding post.

Between Borsh and Lukove, Kadris tells the story of his thirty-four-year-old brother-in-law joining this southward flight. By Kadris's account Romano had a miserable time.

He had almost frozen to death while crossing the Pindus pass in ice and snow. The Albanian border guards had turned their backs by this stage. But on the Greek side, the guards fired at the refugees, and in a panic Romano ran off the track and lost his way. Many hours later, a Greek shepherd picked him up and took care of him. Romano was fed goat milk and cheese. He spent the night with the shepherd, in the lee of a tall stone cairn, listening to the wind lift and whistle off the peaks.

At first light Romano was taken to a village; from there he was handed on down a line of villages, until at the last one, he was shown onto a road.

He walked all the next day and arrived in a village, worn out and scared, and from there he spent all his savings on a single taxi fare to Athens.

He found the centre of Athens crawling with his half-starved countrymen. They roamed the markets scavenging for scraps and fighting one another. It was a terrible time.

Romano was on the brink of starting back home when he landed a part in a film. An Australian crew filming a documentary on the origins of the marathon, in time for the Barcelona Olympics, needed extras—runners. Romano signed on with thirty or forty half-starved Albanians. They were driven in covered army trucks to various places on the outskirts of Athens. Silent with hunger they lined up for singlets and shorts designed after the 1896 Athens Olympics.

For hours at a time, Romano and the other refugees jogged behind a vehicle with a camera mounted on specially built struts. They ran through the suburbs around Athens. One morning they drove far out into the countryside and spent the day running along a hill road. At the end of the day's shoot they changed out of the running gear into their rags and were driven back into the centre of Athens. At night they slept around Omonia Square, one hand clenched around their earnings—ten dollars a day—and in their other hand a knife. In the morning the truck rounded them up again.

After ten days Romano had earned one hundred dollars—and while it was more than he could earn in a year back home, he had had enough.

"Homesick," said Kadris, and he mentioned a wife and daughter.

Romano arrived home with fifty dollars in his pocket, pushing ahead of himself a small fridge on wheels specially fitted for the journey.

38

It is already dark by the time we wind down off the hilltops into Sarandë, on the coast. But even in the dark it is possible to see that Sarandë is deserving of its umbrella logo on Cliff's map. A horseshoe bay begins at one end with a swept-up hotel and stretches round to the port-lit end. On the beach, below the line of pine trees, is a lifeguard tower; no concrete bunkers, none that I can see, anyway.

The lights of Corfu can be seen across the channel. Back in Savra, where I had whiled away the time studying Cliff's map, Sarandë's proximity to Corfu had suggested other possibilities. Food. Drink. "Dollar shops." Coming down from the Llogara Pass I had briefly entertained thoughts of outdoor tables and chairs, somewhere with a menu and plenty of red wine shipped across the border.

Unfortunately, the one hotel open is a dollar one wanting sixty U.S. dollars a night per person, as opposed to the forty cents I had paid in Lushnje.

The woman behind the desk won't entertain leks. She snaps, "Dollars! Dollars!"

It is during the search for an alternative hotel that Sarandë reveals its other, more familiar side. Windows are boarded up. Hotel signs hang broken from a nail. We swoop upon one hotel, boarded up but nonetheless with a light on in its lobby, but no one answers our hammering on the door.

We head back to the dollar hotel and discover that it has a lek restaurant. The menu features just one item, a sweet cake oozing honey which has been trucked in from over the border.

Fortunately, we had managed to eat something earlier, in Lukove, a village sitting high above the beach and with a two-storey restaurant set back from the road. The windows had been blasted out and a very cold wind blew in off the sea. We had the dining room to ourselves. We ate the last of the soup and were watched through a doorway by a room crammed with men lingering over empty coffee cups.

We eat what we can of the cake and I buy the rest for Shapallo, who hadn't wanted to leave the car.

Hoxha's birthplace, Gjirokastër, is another two hours' drive. There is no choice but to push on there and hope for a lek hotel.

As we climb up to the main road, Sarandë drops from view and the back window fills with the lights from Corfu. Soon the last of the lights are well behind us, and it is pitch black. Sometime later we start to lose speed, and begin a long climb that reduces us to a crawl. On one corner a wheel catches a patch of ice; it spins furiously and then we lurch off again.

We probably should have waited until morning. We could have slept in the car. Our headlights have started to pick up snowdrifts, and as we grind it out around steep bends, the lights disconcertingly vanish into a black chasm.

I ask Kadris if he has any idea of how high the mountain is.

"Very, very high."

He leans forward to confer, but Mentor has no idea either.

"Tell him to change down."

"I have told him this already. Many, many times. Mentor does not enjoy the sound of those gears."

Then he checks with Shapallo, who is none the wiser either. But as Shapallo tilted his head back, in the dashlights I'd caught that side profile of the Emperor—"like Orson Welles," one British Special Operations agent had written in his report. Hoxha reminded another of a "seedy student."

In the dashlight it is Shapallo's doggy grin, that expression of knowingness that he has had to carry around with him ever since Tef shoved him out into a world where at the mere sight of him farmworkers had dropped their picks and hay rakes.

The other night, relating these difficulties, Shapallo had compared the Sun King's experiences to his own. He had read that first-time visitors to Louis's court were often advised to get used to seeing the King before raising the courage to address him, since first contact with his personality often struck them dumb. In the early days before he grew a beard and disfigured himself, farmworkers, woodcutters, agronomists, children, muleteers—all had stopped in their tracks at the sight of Shapallo shambling towards them. Old men rubbed at their eyes. Children looked around and ran for it.

Once, in the fields outside Seman, I think it was, in Apollonia, Shapallo tried to convince a farmworker that he was not a ghost. But the man stuck out his hands to prevent Shapallo from venturing any closer.

I imagine a smiling beneficence had seen Shapallo through. The sea of bewildered faces parting, the landscape opening up, and Shapallo, both amused and regretful, like the condemned actor forever remembered for just one role, taking his resigned grin off in the direction of the darkening range of hills.

One night earlier this year he had entered a village to look for food and found Enver's statue toppled in the square. His first thoughts were to hold an act of God responsible. He looked closer. Enver's arms were tied behind his back, and painted over the raised cheek was the word mut, or shit.

A week later, near Elbasan, he had picked up a news-paper used by a truck driver to wipe his hands after changing a tyre, and there, beneath oily thumbprints, was a photo-graph of "hooligans" swarming into Embassy Row.

I seem to recall that back in Tirana virtually every black-market commodity carried a Greek label. People spoke of the "highway" up from Greece and I had imagined lanes of traffic and convoys of trucks travelling through the night.

But the highway I had expected is a country road. Down the other side of the mountain we arrive at a junction: an-other five kilometres south lies the Greek border; eighteen kilometres in the opposite direction is Gjirokastër.

We're the only traffic, and the only change from the jackknifing road which brought us over the mountain is that it now has fewer bends. A moment ago, the headlights picked up the black skin of a river and we've stuck beside it since.

We pass under small villages stapled to the hillside above the road. Sometimes we catch a solitary light. But most of the way is covered in darkness before the start of the con-crete housing blocks announce "new Gjirokastër." The whereabouts of "old Gjirokastër" are a mystery.

We have to wind down the windows to listen for sounds of habitation, more like woodsmen than motorists with a map. A light snow is falling and we can hear the dull sounds of an axe biting into damp wood. Then Kadris sights a tiny cluster of glowworm lights high, high above the road.

We climb to a grand-looking hotel that sits at the foot of the old fortress walls; then the road closes up to a cobbled lane full of sharp bends and exquisite wood and lead-light boutiques. Here is the imprimatur of private ownership. A pipe shop. A bar. A bakery. None open at this hour, but a heartening sight nonetheless.

We have zigzagged our way to an area above the fortress walls to find the house of the local Democrat leader, an old university buddy of Kadris's. The snow is falling heavily and the prospect of a night sitting upright in the Volvo is a daunting one.

Kadris's friend, like all the other Democrats I have met, is an economics teacher. A dark, slim man in his early thirties. In the hotel the Democrat takes the hand of a rather formidable woman behind the desk and coaxes from her an acceptable deal—Kadris, Mentor, and Shapallo will pay in leks, but I must pay in dollars, in advance.

There are signs pointing to the dining room; another promises a bar. But the only voices we hear are our own. The Democrat apologises for everything having closed down so early. But the hotel staff fear for their security.

Gjirokastër, Brikena had told me, was an "intellectual town."

"There is also the possibility of vandalism and windows getting smashed," continues the Democrat.

"But why?"

"Debate. Argument," he says. "It is the biggest problem for our party to explain that after fifty years of unified Party stand on everything, healthy debate is not the same thing as anarchy."

We have two rooms at the end of a long, carpeted corridor. We are the only guests on the second floor. Miraculously the rooms are heated. The shower works. There is hot water! And a fluffy eiderdown on each bed. I drift off, watching the snow fall on an owl sitting on a bare branch in the window.

39

Last night's hopes of finding food have come to nothing. This morning we were late getting downstairs and the restaurant had run out of bread.

On a more pleasant note Gjirokastër is beautiful. I think Enver must have drawn the line here, since the grubby housing blocks, like an invading army, have got no farther than the bottom of the hill.

Outside, it is pure mountain air. Shapallo has his coat collar pushed up around his ears—not sure as to what he would value more at this moment, a cup of coffee or total invisibility. On the way to Enver's house we stop at a shop filled with Greek merchandise and sightseers. I buy some brandy and chocolate, and a scarf for Shapallo.

The mountain behind Gjirokastër is buried in a grey mist. Underfoot are pink and grey bricks. The houses are the colour of old snow. The slate on their roofs is a dark, wet grey. Outside each house people have lit small fires under their frozen water pipes.

We find Enver's old house easily enough. For years it was a shrine; now, we discover it is an archive.

This morning a boy of sixteen or seventeen guards the door. In his hands he has a rifle dating back to the partisans' campaigns. His tousled brown hair is filled with snowflakes, which have been falling all morning. His eyes and nose are running. His hands are numb with cold.

Kadris gives him a piece of chocolate, and for the moment the rifle dangles like a shoulder bag while he licks his fingers.

We slip in the door and immediately come up against a second line of defence, a well-dressed woman who has managed to escape the usual drab custodian's uniform. The conversation runs a predictable course. First the official line—it is quite impossible for anyone to visit, since the archive is closed.

"Yes, yes, of course," says Kadris; then he asks me for a dollar.

The woman quickly pockets it. But she is not particularly pleased to have done so. She has some harsh words for the boy soldier, who, covered with shame, returns to his post with his chocolate fingers.

The invitation is to look. We must not touch the cartons. A few minutes is all she will allow. Time, she says, "to soak up the atmosphere." The woman's mutterings chase us up the stairs.

One wall has been devoted to a photographic display, and Shapallo is most interested in this. There is Enver, the studious youth. Enver at the beach, where the future leader with the "film-star looks" already seems inordinately aware of the camera, more so than he is of the sun on his shoulders and back.

There is the famous smile which at a glance was said to have ripened fruit; this same thing for which women forgave his occasional rudeness.

The photograph that has interested Shapallo so much is

one of Enver standing with a group of comrades. Enver is the only one not listening to the photographer's instructions. The rest of the comrades smile into the lens, whereas Enver, arms folded, is uncharacteristically glancing off to somewhere in the wings.

Something has caught his attention, and fifty years later in a different time and place he and Shapallo appear to be exchanging glances: youth contemplating old age or, just as likely, old age glancing back down the same road.

We move along to the oil paintings—most of them studies of Lenin kindly listening to the problems of peasants; or at his writing desk, in a pensive mood, smiling at the brilliant thought still to be completed on the sheet of paper.

The oil studies of Lenin are succeeded by a photograph of the "bookish" Enver studying at Montpellier University; books pile up on a corner of his desk. A pipe smoulders away at his elbow.

We stop before a glass-framed article from L'Humanité, the French Communist Party newspaper. The thing confusing Shapallo is the byline of Lulo Malessori, the pseudonym behind which Enver had unleashed his attacks against King Zog.

The custodian explains this to Shapallo, and the matter of Zog's withdrawal of Enver's scholarship at Montpellier. Enver's shift to Paris; his brief sojourn in Belgium.

But it is only the pseudonym which interests Shapallo, this confection of another identity which had left Enver free to explore a different kind of life. He is completely entranced.

The custodian is directing searching glances towards the stairs and checking her watch. She tries to take Shapallo's elbow, but he won't budge from this remnant of Enver's life as Lulo Malessori.

The woman appeals to Kadris. We really shouldn't be here. It was an exceptional circumstance.

"Please," she says.

Kadris takes Shapallo by the arm, and the woman pushes him from behind down the stairs.

There are some sharp words for the boy-soldier blowing on his frozen fingers, and the door cracks behind us.

Snowflakes melt on the pink and grey cobblestones. The smoking grey slate rooftops have grown darker.

40

Palli Kuke tells the story of filming Enver during one of his last visits to Gjirokastër.

Enver had come to visit with an old relative and Palli's job was to get footage of the prodigal son returned home sitting in a relative's back yard. The Secret Police had already been through the place. The water had been tested, the coffee had been prepared well in advance, and the cameras began to film Enver at leisure.

Everything was proceeding nicely. The Great Leader was halfway through telling this woman, his relative, that despite the years marching on they were both still very strong.

But the woman refused to humour him.

"No, no," she said. "We are so very old."

Enver smiled tolerantly. "Why," he said, "I will live to be one hundred."

"No, no!" cried the old crone. "I tell you, we are all finished!"

Ramiz and Nexhmije exchanged anxious looks. Palli kept his eye hard against the lens. He could feel the tension among the aides and the variously employed Secret Police. Everyone was panicking as to what would happen next.

There was no way to stop that old woman until Ramiz skilfully intervened. To everyone's relief Ramiz said to Enver, "Of course you will live to one hundred, because that is in your family line. But you will get another twenty years from socialism."

Everyone immediately relaxed and applauded Ramiz's promise to Enver that he would live to the ripe old age of one hundred and twenty.

41

Before leaving Gjirokastër I had bought some Greek beer and we drank it while tracking a river valley the thirty kilometres to Tepelenë. Mentor had the car heater billowing warm air to the back and everyone was in a good mood, glad to be out of the weather, and soon the bottles were rolling on the floor, back and forth, under our feet.

We had left behind the snow clouds and everything was grey and purple, with streaks of green pasture sown among rocks on the valley sides. Shapallo said this was how Topojani had appeared in his thoughts over the years.

In spring, after the last rains, the women picked herbs off the rocks. Shapallo's Topojani resisted the usual seasonal changes. It was always spring. In spring the children were always leading the goats and sheep back up to higher ground to nibble at the green wet from the melted snow. The bumps in the road made his head jog with happy memories.

He laughed aloud one time, opening his eyes with surprise. He reeled something off in a hurry, and Kadris dutifully passed on that "Mister Shapallo had temporarily lost himself in Topojani."

A few kilometres later, Shapallo asked if we could carry on to Tirana. He said he would like to see Munz.

After that Mentor drove like an old nag with its nose turned for home. We sped through Tepelenë, a grey nondescript village where Lord Byron, in 1809, had spent a few nights as the guest of Ali Pasha. The pasha had praised Byron's small, delicate fingers. In return Byron had been moved to write of the virility of the people in "Childe Harold":

Where is the foe that ever saw their back?
Who can so well the toil of war endure?

South of Fier we strike the oilfields. Partly congealed oil slicks dribble into slack rivers, and before a factory wall with a beautiful mural of paradise, a Chinese truck rests on its axles.

We catch up with some traffic, Russian and Chinese trucks filled to the gunwales with secondhand washing machines and fridges, and rugs. The passengers squat down in the back between appliances, red-eyed and miserable with cold. All of them with towels wrapped around their heads from crossing the icy passes between Greece and Albania, earlier in the day.

The way is flat and featureless. Men warming their

gloved hands over small fires on the shingle flats look up at our passing.

By early afternoon we are back on the road between Fier and Lushnje. Rising above the unsown fields is Savra, grey and slab-like. In a few minutes we are tearing past, Shapallo with his arms folded and his eyelids at half-mast.

Now, without any need to stop at Savra, I just want to get it over with and get back to Tirana. To get over the yawning familiarity of the countryside. The gaunt figures pedalling across flat farm paths. The dismal light and the bitten-down roadside stumps.

"Kavajë," announces Mentor.

He raises his hands off the steering wheel to await instructions. Kadris waves him on.

We had gone through Lushnje the same way, feeling like fugitives, no one quite able to bring himself to mention Leila and Guria, or Doctor Cabey sitting alone in his study with his stuffed birds. I thought of Mister Gina, his sadly etched face rallying to a smile in the small aperture of our back window.

We reached the Durrës/Tirana junction with the last of the daylight. Another thirty minutes and a tidal ring of abandoned factories and the first of Tirana's housing blocks popped up. We were all dozing when Mentor braked suddenly for a cart and horse. While we slid across the road, the horse-and-cart driver trotted on, the back of the driver's head and the rear of the horse's arse bobbing together.

Mentor switched on the engine and there was a terrible noise of loose metal parts being shaken up in a can—and that was the end of the gear box.

He sprung the bonnet, but the engine was lost in the dark and poor, wretched Mentor leant his head against the raised lid. He refused to leave the car. He worried that if he deserted it here overnight it would be picked clean and left a corpse. We left him in his car and walked silently for about ten minutes, before a bus pulled over.

Shortly after, we arrived in Tirana, careering into Skanderbeg Square like every other bus I had seen arrive—spectacularly, as though arriving in an arena, the whole body swaying on broken suspension and spilling all the passengers to one side of the bus—an old man with just two teeth grinned inches from my face. Something soft pushed against my groin. I looked down and in the old man's hands was a duck, large, white, and composed like the ones I had seen in Fier, tied to bicycle carriers.

The bus lurched to a stop. Together with the old man and his duck I fell through the doors.

Kadris held on to Shapallo's arm and helped him down.

Across the square the sea of money changers bobbed up to the doors of the Tirana Hotel. Opposite the darkened Palace of Culture the lights were on in the mosque. From a first-floor window in the side of the museum building, a tired tape of Michael Jackson's *Bad* blared over the heads of the money changers. In a completely unexpected way Tirana felt welcoming, even exhilarating. The lights were out—the result of yet another power cut—but the people were abroad in numbers, hopeful and expectant of something happening.

Kadris was laughing—Shapallo had wanted to know what had become of Enver. There was a hole in the night where the eighteen-foot statue had previously stood and Shapallo wanted to wander over and inspect the curled-up tear in the metal.

I said to Kadris, "Let's get a beer at the Dajti."

We had to push Shapallo through the various zones, past the fringe of begging gypsy children, the expensive red taxis, the soldiers who stood on the hotel steps as if it were the Presidential Palace, through the revolving doors into a lobby crowded with smoke and talk.

Kadris went to tighten the knot in his tie, as always mindful of his tidy appearance. But I noticed a layer of grime around his white collar, and the cuffs of his trousers were caked with dried mud from Savra. I hadn't shaved once in all the time away from here. My skin hadn't seen a cake of soap either.

A waitress carrying a fax on a silver tray passed under Shapallo's nose with a look of disgust.

There were women with fur stoles. Men with shiny black shoes and buttoned-up coats. Businessmen from the former bloc countries rocked on their heels, their thin lips unable to suppress the delight they felt at the longing, around them, for their sharp clothes. These intensely felt jealousies of a high-school prom attached to every glance.

Conversation hummed along in half a dozen languages. But one familiar voice singled itself out. His back was turned to me. The elbows of his ski jacket fanned out as his hands circled the air.

"They do this veal croquette thing. You know, done up in bread crumbs and butter. And some kind of antipasto with eggplant I'm sure they stole from someplace. Tomatoes, chives, olives . . . with a little Parmesan sprinkled."

One of the aid people caught my eye, said something, and Bill turned at the elbow. He turned all the way round, then squinted through his spectacles.

"Hey," he said. "There you are!"

Then he held out a hand and I introduced Kadris and Shapallo, and Bill said, "Oh yeah, glad to meet you."

42

We were in Tirana only another four days, but in that time we ran about like tourists.

On the second morning back, I walked Kadris across town to the railway station. We'd been in touch with Mentor the previous day. His car was waiting for parts to be sent by his nephew in Italy. In the meantime, he had returned home and was paying a neighbour fifty leks a night to sleep in the car and keep watch.

I was sorry to see Kadris go, but he had a wife and a four-year-old child waiting for him back in Lushnje. Before leaving he introduced me to one of his former English students, Diani, who worked in the university publishing house. Diani was a small, feisty bundle of energy who lived with her soccer-coach husband in an apartment towards the bottom end of the Boulevard of Martyrs.

She had clapped her hands and yelped with excitement when she learned I had been in Kukës.

"Did you find it beautiful? Oh, and the lake," she said. "It is my favourite place in all of Albania."

She described where she had lived there, in one of the

apartments near the playground with the rusted Ferris wheel. On the other side of the playground was a soccer field, and her apartment overlooked that.

"Kukës is where I met Raffi," she said. "I used to stand on my balcony and watch him kick the ball."

Kadris and I said our goodbyes. He promised to look out for Leila. On the steps of the bus he had another inspiration. Perhaps even take her some food?

His bus started to fill up and Kadris disappeared under a cargo of boxes and poultry, and I was able to slip away.

With Munz and Shapallo, one afternoon we found Shapallo's old house. A German oil executive was living there now. His wife answered the door but refused us entry. So we stood in the garden and Shapallo had to place for us the dull earthenware pot that had brimmed with sweet Williams. We stood before the wall where the soldiers had stood, and where in summer faint brown clouds of insects hovered overhead, stuck in the aroma of the banana-fruit nectar and wisteria.

He and Munz got along in French.

Shapallo said to Munz, "I don't remember these curtains." We turned to the window. Shapallo waved and the oil executive's wife pulled a face. A light rain began to fall and Munz put his arm through Shapallo's to hurry him along.

Shetitone Donika Kastrioti is the rruga on the very perimeter of the block, divided from the Boulevard of Martyrs by a park with the triple busts of the patriots from whom the rruga takes its name. We were walking there, past the Italian villas and ministries, when Munz pointed out Enver's son-in-law. He was one of a number of men lounging out-side the wrought-iron fence of one of the villas.

I hadn't given much thought to the Hoxha family. Be-sides Nexhmije, I knew Enver had left behind two sons and a daughter. I had assumed that they had fled the country. As for Nexhmije, in Shkodër I had heard her variously ru-moured as dead, exiled to Greece, or living in great luxury in Paris.

Munz laughed dismissively.

"Nexhmije is alive and well. In fact, she is living in this very street."

"No."

"Yes. Why not? I don't know the exact house, but it is in this street."

Shapallo stood detached, his hands clasped behind his back and without much of a clue as to what we were talking about.

"She is in this street," Munz continued, and then broke away. He caught up with a woman leaving the gate of a villa up ahead.

Munz explained that the woman was from the Libyan embassy.

She nodded to a three-storey white slab building next door to the Libyans.

"Yes. That is Nexhmije," she said.

It all seemed so improbably easy. I looked back in the direction we had come, but the son-in-law had disappeared.

I said to Munz, "Is she sure?"

"Yes, of course." He added, "Nexhmije's whereabouts are no great secret, at least, not in Tirana."

The woman from the embassy was eager to help. She

ran back inside to retrieve a telephone number, but returned apologetic. The number she had was the old one for the former Hoxha compound.

I asked Munz to check just one last time. The reply was sharp: "Nexhmije! Yes, I have seen her for myself."

The white building gave nothing away. On every floor the curtains were drawn. Munz read my thoughts and chuckled. "Another time."

We wandered across the park opposite the Dajti and took shelter under a tree out of the drizzle. A man had driven his Fiat into the artificial lake and was washing it down with soapy water. A steady breeze blew the suds across the lake to the far side.

Munz thought it would be a good idea for Shapallo to visit Enver's tomb, so we took one of the red taxis up to the shrine, which overlooks the city.

It was more exposed on the knoll, and the soldiers guarding Enver's remains blew on their fingers. They complained to Shapallo about the low pay they got compared to the ordinary police, who they claimed received special cigarette and raki allowances on top of their regular wage. They were a discontented lot. Guarding Enver's bones was not the job it used to be.

In the past, when the relieving shift came on, the old shift had to depart, walking backwards, and without taking their eyes off the tomb until the new guard was in place. But a slackness had slipped into the job ever since Enver's statue in Skanderbeg Square had been hauled down and urinated on. It was a curious conversation, which Shapallo relayed back through Munz, as the soldiers spoke about a loss of pride and the low morale which had entered the job.

Shapallo wandered around the tomb. He was a good deal more interested in Enver's burial place than he had been in the house in which he had spent all those years as Enver's double. At one point he placed a foot on the tomb and a soldier was sufficiently moved to stamp out his cigarette and with his rifle steer Shapallo back to a respectful distance.

It was during the ride back to Munz's apartment, where Shapallo was staying, that he started to discuss with Munz the Sun King's death. It was all passed on by a startled Munz: how, at the moment of death, Louis's bedchamber had been turned into a butcher shop. Shapallo, as was his wont at such times, spoke slowly and assuredly, like a lecturer, shaping his sentences and stacking them on end with the palms of his hands.

The butchering was standard practice, explained Shapallo. The surgeons carrying out the autopsy had discovered that half the Sun King's upper jawbone was missing. The dissection further revealed evidence of a prodigious appetite: a huge royal stomach and intestines, twice the normal length. A tight-fitting shoe when finally pried from one foot had those gathered around Louis's bedchamber gagging on the foul smell of gangrenous flesh.

Munz said to me, "I had not heard him speak of Louis before."

But Shapallo was not finished. Munz sat back and he continued. He had sometimes wondered, he said, had he intercepted a bullet during those years he was the Emperor's decoy, and were he subjected to the same intense autopsy as Louis, whether his captors would have found stamped over his grey matter a town plan of Topojani, with every cottage and family represented.

Later that evening I found Munz waiting for me down in the lobby. As I approached he said, "I think he wants to go back."

Topojani wasn't on Cliff's map, but Bill had heard of it. "Remote. Difficult," he said.

Topojani was one of the villages on Mustaph's circuit. A week before our visit to Kukës, Mustaph had tried with a truck to get to Topojani but had found the road washed away.

"Who's wanting to go?" he asked.

"Petar Shapallo."

"That old guy? You mean the guy you were telling me about?" He smiled. "No shit."

Then he thought for a moment. "If you can wait a couple of days. We've got a 'shoe drop' planned for Shishtavec. It's up on the border. If we don't get there soon we won't at all because of winter. Leave it with me," he said.

43

Nexhmije is living above a customs house. I made this discovery when I returned this morning, with Diani, to the building next door to the Libyans.

The neglect so evident outside the block had found its way inside Nexhmije's new address. In the courtyard weeds sprouted around broken bits of concrete, and around the back of the building an old car crouched on flat tyres.

A crowd stood in the drizzle up to the back door. Diani was a little terrier. She shouldered her way through and collared the boy on the door.

We hustled through and the boy closed the door after us. We found ourselves in a stairwell littered with rubbish. I could see down the stairs to the basement, where aid parcels from relatives living overseas had arrived. Scrawled over the cream walls were: BORN WILD, BLAZE OF GLORY, STING.

"You want Nexhmije?" The boy pointed up the stairs. Then he bounced ahead in his jeans and on the second floor knocked on the door with youthful impudence.

"It's Alban. Open the door!" Then he started to call out for "Aunty Nexhmije."

A woman's voice answered on the other side. After further exchanges, the door opened to a cautious gap and the face of an old house servant appeared. She looked me up and down. Then she told Diani that Nexhmije was busy at this moment and that we should return at five o'clock with the proper documentation.

A letter from Cliff was my only introduction. He had written on a "Friends of Albania" letterhead asking that the Albanian authorities extend every courtesy to me. In Rome, when the consul had asked for something other than my passport, I had offered Cliff's letter and then nervously looked on as the consul's eye travelled down the page to nod with approval at Cliff's presidential signature.

By four o'clock it is already dark and the rain which has threatened all day is bucketing down. Another power cut has plunged the city into darkness. The money changers have been dispersed indoors. The gypsy beggars have given up for the day. Just the rifle barrels stick out in the rain from the doorways of the government buildings.

We plunge through empty streets ankle deep in surface water. The concrete drain or canal which bisects Tirana is roaring in the dark.

There are a few grey vans parked on Shetitone Donika Kastrioti; otherwise the rain has driven indoors the soldiers who usually stand in the gardens. We enter Nexhmije's gate and wade through puddles to the back of the customs house. The rain has whittled the crowd down, but a brave lot remains pushed up to the door under umbrellas. I can smell their wet hair as they part to let the foreigner through.

Alban has been waiting for us. The door opens and closes like a bivalve and we wriggle through. The stairs are lost in darkness. The smell of wet cardboard points to the customs house. Fortunately Alban has a torch, and we follow the spotlight up the stairs.

I notice that this time he knocks on the door with more respect. He flicks off his torch and we wait in the fetid dark for the footsteps on the wooden floor to reach the door.

The door opens and warm oven smells of roasted meat precede a large, balding man in his mid-thirties. He has large feminine eyes in a soft, round, cheerful face. He looks nothing like Enver or, for that matter, Shapallo. This is Illir, Nexhmije's youngest son.

He speaks a little English, but after we exchange a few pleasantries, it dries up.

I hand over Cliff's letter, and Illir takes Alban's torch and reads it on the landing. Near the end of Cliff's salutations and presidential signature, Illir smiles good-naturedly.

"You have Albanians living in New Zealand?"

Diani takes it upon herself to explain, in a high screeching voice, "Illir wishes to know. This letter is from the Albanian Society . . ."

"Yes. Yes. We have some Albanians."

Illir begins to fold the letter. "May I?" he asks. He would like to hold on to Cliff's letter for now.

For the next few minutes he and Diani discuss something. Apparently we had been expected, but Illir regrets to have to tell us that his mother has not yet returned. However, he does not anticipate a problem. If we call at a later date he feels sure that his mother will agree to an interview.

While Alban aims his torch, Illir takes my notebook and scribbles down his telephone number.

"Please ring before you visit next time," he says.

We shake hands and he retreats inside the door to finish his dinner.

Outside the customs house the rain is even heavier than before, but neither of us is bothered by it. Diani waits until we are well past the grey van before she shows her excitement. The other occasions she had seen Illir were on television, but never, as she puts it, "to share the same air."

"I have done well?" she asks.

"Extremely well."

"You will tell this to Kadris, of course."

She waits, and in the dark comes a high peal of laughter.

"I am so very happy for you," she says. "You are going to meet Nexhmije."

———

Brikena was surprised. She refused to believe Nexhmije was living unprotected.

"We didn't see a single soul," I said.

"Ah yes, but they would have seen you. Definitely. Nexhmije is a very powerful woman. No one can touch her."

Brikena had read in that morning's *Democratic Renaissance* of Liliana Hoxha, the wife of the older son, Solkol, threatening her critics. Liliana is the vice-director of the Albanian News Agency, and one of her critics, a trade unionist, had been confronted by six armed thugs and told, "If you go on talking about Liliana Hoxha we will liquidate your family and children."

The implication was that if Liliana could muster a gang of thugs, then Nexhmije could surround herself with an army.

"You know," said Brikena, "there were rumours that the Hoxha family celebrated when news came through of the coup against Gorbachev."

A couple of days later, Diani took me to the Expo on the ground floor of the Enver Hoxha Memorial. A crowd six deep scrimmaged around a rock video of Prince and his sunglassed blondes. The Czechs had arrived with electronic equipment and chocolates. Everything was ticketed in American "doolars." The Hungarians had sent six pairs of shoes and attractive posters of the Danube. The disembodied bus turned out to be theirs. Diani was very impressed by the fact of a bus's having got inside a building. It was a bit like a ship in a bottle, she struggled to explain. Good-naturedly she waved up at a number of Albanians who gazed demurely out the windows, perhaps imagining a passing landscape in the West. Space for the Romanian exhibit had been roped off, but the floor area was bereft of merchandise. Instead, a man dressed in a black suit stood next to a tape deck playing Romanian music.

Our appointment was up on the next floor with the chief engineer, an amateur filmmaker who had filmed Enver's only moment of exile.

Gone was the soaring choral music of the official version. On the chief engineer's video was the sound of hammers chipping away at Enver's bulk. The builders were barefoot and wore pointed paper hats.

The engineer explained that it had been planned to preserve the statue as a work of art, that different strategies to relocate Hoxha had been considered, but in every case the plan involved destroying part of the museum to get him out. Finally it was decided to preserve Enver's head and shoulders.

On the video the upper body was clearly supposed to slide forward onto a ready tray, but the weight of the head had been miscalculated and the bust toppled backwards. On impact, the head broke off and rolled loose.

On the engineer's video there was an astonished silence. The camera remained fixed on the head, as if to make sure of the fact. You could hear cameras clicking. Then a length of plywood was slipped underneath Enver's head, the way you gingerly remove dog crap from the lawn.

It was in marked contrast, sobering even, after a morning spent in the company of the Sun King, to then run across the same man's son. Particularly when the latter was so much part of the crowd, rolling along with his hands dumped in the pockets of his leather jacket.

This was on the bridge near the Dajti, where Diani and I were sunning ourselves. Over Illir's shoulder was the shrine to his Brahman father.

Away from the bad light of the stairwell, I noticed again the roundness of his head and the feminine eyelashes. Illir seemed so harmless—which Diani later said was exactly how his father had come across: a friendly wave to the crowd; his bending to receive the flower bouquet from the small girl, a pat on the head and smiling back at the camera.

Illir glanced at his watch. He had an appointment, but he accepted an invitation to have coffee in the Dajti.

For once the foyer and lounge were nearly empty. A lovely day must have cleared the usual denizens outdoors. The waitress who set down the tray with the coffees showed no recognition of Illir. For his part, he was perfectly relaxed.

In light of the recent boat exodus we talked about "travel," Illir's favourite places. As director of the Mechanics Institute he had got around: Italy. Germany. Italy. Sweden. Stockholm remained his favourite place.

"Oh?"

"Stockholm was very nice."

And that was Stockholm.

Illir remained wary—he turned innocent questions around in his head. Whenever in doubt he presented a banal smile. But he did mention that his mother, as of this moment, was at a court hearing into financial abuses by the former "block men."

Of course, he said, it was all political. Farcical really. He laughed. We were to understand that the investigation was

a bit of nonsense which Nexhmije, in her sleep, would fold
into a dart and throw away.

44

Bill had heard from Mustaph that snow
was dusting the hills around Kukës. Soon the outlying villages would be buried and the roads, such as they were,
would disappear altogether.

Meanwhile, the "big guy" had started to worry Bill. He
wanted assurances that Shapallo was "legal."

"Stuff like contraband, and my ass will be kicked from
here to the moon," he said.

I promised him Shapallo wasn't "contraband."

"I meant that just as an example. Understand?"

It had become too dangerous for an aid vehicle to drive
at night. Desperately hungry people were looting warehouses out in the countryside, and Bill guessed the same
ones were responsible for rolling trees across the road after
dark.

Teti was missing from the team. Bill had acted on his
word and sacked him. But Teti hadn't gone without a struggle. First Teti's mother, then his sister, had knocked on Bill's
door with various cakes and sweet things.

"The mother made me this coconut kind of cake with a
syrup you wouldn't believe. I shouldn't have accepted it,"
he said. "I shouldn't have. You know, I nearly took him
back? Can you believe that? I swear to God I nearly took
him back." He shook his head in wonder.

We didn't leave until eight in the morning. Bill hunched over the wheel, with his pipe, and Anila alongside, wrapped in her fur coat, gritting her teeth at song after song out of Nashville.

It was a dull kind of day. The skies were lower and everything felt compressed. Towns popped up in quick succession and we sped through them like sleepless truck drivers.

Near Carrik the tape deck fell silent for a period. Bill jammed his knee under the steering wheel to get his pipe lit. "How we doing back there?" he asked.

Otherwise, Shapallo and I were pretty much left on our own. A couple of times Shapallo started to mention something. He leant forward to get Anila's attention, his hand hovered above Anila's cool shoulder, but then he seemed to think better of it and swallowed whatever he had intended to say. After that, he sat back, closed his eyes, and dozed.

Early in the afternoon we started the long descent into Kukës. On the far side of the valley the hilltops carried the snow Mustaph had spoken of, and now Shapallo sat up and started to take notice. As we neared the town he twisted about anxiously, swapping the side-window view for the one out the rear, and mumbling to himself.

Anila lolled her head on the backrest and in her tired way explained, "Mister Shapallo does not believe me that this is Kukës."

Shapallo shook his head, very deliberately.

"Did you tell him this is new Kukës?"

"I have said this already."

"Tell him old Kukës is under water."

Now she turned around for the old man's attention and explained the rising of the lake.

Immediately Shapallo began to look around for the lake. It was no use telling him. Bill put off Mustaph for the time being and drove to a vantage point near the hotel high above the lake, where we parked and got out of the Land Cruiser. Shapallo could not believe it. A vast silver lacquer covered everything he had remembered about Kukës. The faintest of breezes stirred the lake, and yet, somehow, the same breeze sliced with remarkable ease through our layers of clothing.

For quite a while Shapallo shook his head at the lake and smacked his lips the way he had when he discovered Enver's giant statue gone from Skanderbeg Square. He started to wheeze, and his breathing became ragged. He couldn't take his eyes off the lake. He was quite mesmerised. The rest of us had got back in the Land Cruiser, Anila with her hands held up to the fan heater.

Bill was first to notice that Shapallo was not quite himself. He pulled him back in the van. Shapallo's head fell back when he sat down, and Bill raised his eyes.

"We just gave him a helluva shock."

Now Shapallo was babbling away again, as if talking in his sleep.

Anila chewed gum and listened.

"Mister Shapallo is talking about photographs." She stopped chewing. "Photographs. That is all he is saying. He cannot go back to Topojani without the photographs." She stopped to listen again. "I don't know. I think perhaps he is saying this."

We drove to the hotel and booked in. With Anila's help we got Shapallo upstairs to a room on the second floor which looked across to the hillside slogan PARTI ENVER and the copper smelter. We manoevred Shapallo onto the bed and pulled his shoes off, then covered him up. His teeth were chattering with cold. Anila found an extra blanket. Shapallo closed his eyes and raised a hand to say he was okay.

While there was still enough daylight Bill and I decided to take a run across to the start of the gorge. It's ten minutes' drive to the hillside, then the road passes underneath the copper smelter. The road dips and meets up with the river, which is every bit as fast and furious as the river Shapallo had described. It is only halfway across the bridge that you become aware of the gorge wending its way to the frontier. Suddenly limestone walls rise to hundreds of feet either side of the river, their tops buried in a thick grey mist.

We bounce along a road which sticks to the left side of the river. Out my window there's no road to speak of, just a sheer drop to white and brown rapids rushing out to the plains.

Every hundred metres or so the gorge discloses a little more of itself, each bend seeming to isolate us further from the late twentieth century. We catch up with some women in traditional dress. Further ahead, there are some men and small undernourished boys with caps and in hand-me-down army uniforms worn casually like overalls.

We don't seem to be climbing, but soon the river is reduced to a muddy, squiggling thread. Above, the limestone cliffs are smudged with mist.

Bill is driving with his headlights on now. Around one corner the lights trap a woman butchering a calf on the side of the road.

"Holy shit," says Bill. "Did you see?"

We had slowed to walking pace, and as we passed the woman she was holding the calf by its ears while sawing at its bloody throat.

The walls of the gorge narrow down—never farther apart than the distance you could throw a stone. Then we start to drop, and drop until we meet up with the river again.

Another twenty minutes and we realise we're on our way to Zapod on the Yugoslav border. We've come to a smashed wooden bridge dangling in the rapids, right where the river falls in great bucketfuls over smooth round boulders. We backtrack and find a turnoff and start the climb for Shishtavec at six thousand feet.

It is completely dark now, but continuing to show up in the headlights are stragglers carrying loaves and sacks over their shoulders. They push through the milky fog; then these ghosts fall back into darkness. God only knows how they avoid walking off the road and falling to their deaths.

Soon, we come across a group of men loading donkeys with heavy sacks. As the wheel hits a rock the headlights leap up the hillside to where a number of donkeys are making their way up a vertical zigzag, to disappear into the fog.

We push on, Bill with his pipe clenched in his teeth and craning over the wheel. We can't see more than ten feet ahead. The road turns and twists round a coil in the mountain, and up ahead there appear four lights in the fog.

No sooner do these lights appear than we break through the cloudline and suddenly it's as though the fog below us has completely lifted. On the other side of the gorge is the kind of view which you might see from an aeroplane: the lights of a village, not so much in a tight cluster but spread out like brilliant stars in a night sky. And this, too, feels like a completely new world from the one we have just left behind in the gorge.

"Let's see where the hell we are," Bill says.

He switches on the radio, and the next thing we're listening to Miles Davis playing "Five Minutes to Midnight."

"That'll be Yugoslavia," he says.

45

In the morning we return to the gorge— this time with Mustaph and Anila, but without Shapallo.

Shapallo woke complaining of chest pains and nausea. He said he hadn't slept a wink. At breakfast he ate a cold chip, took a sip of coffee, and pushed his chair out.

We helped him back to his room. He was very emotional. His eyes were moist and he shook his head all the way up the stairs. He couldn't understand what had got into him.

Bill told Shapallo there would be another day. "Listen, we can do it another time," he said. "Anila, tell him."

But she refused to; she walked to the window and hissed at Bill, "Can't you see Mister Shapallo does not wish to go?"

But Bill, I think, was just offering up words to smooth over any embarrassment the old man might feel for his loss of nerve after having come this far.

We left Shapallo exactly the way we had yesterday, lying on his bed, his hand raised to signal that all was okay. He had given instructions to Anila that I was to report everything back to him.

"Mister Shapallo wishes to compare pictures," she said.

On the way through we pick up Mustaph; still the same proud figure in a grey coat and buttoned-up shirt. But the gorge this morning is a different place. The sun is out, and streaks of purple and green have replaced yesterday's greys and charcoals. Patches of tilled earth cling tenaciously to the tops of cliffs which, yesterday, were lost in fog.

This morning there is a stronger, more satisfying sense of the gorge leading to somewhere. Far above are large stone houses with slate roofs trailing pale blue smoke.

Yesterday, when we crossed the river, we missed the turnoff winding up the side of the gorge to some rooftops just peeping above a knoll. By Bill's reckoning, Topojani was the starlit village we had looked down upon.

We follow the track for another kilometre until we are high above the river, and across the other side of the gorge we can make out ridges that flatten out to gentler areas for goats and sheep to graze upon. Bill stops to admire the view. "You know," he says, "a smart operator could turn this into a great backpacker's kind of thing. You could make an itinerary and walk along the ridges between villages."

"Fine," snaps Anila. "You come here for your vacation. I will go to Washington for mine."

Anila passes this on to Mustaph and his head rocks back. Amused at first, and then dismayed after he has thought about it some more.

A few minutes on, and we all pile out of the Land

Cruiser. Mustaph. Me. Bill. Anila, with a cool regard for the muddy ground ahead of us.

We are near the top of the rise, and the first slate roofs blink in the hard sunlight. A short climb and Shapallo's village comes into view. Stone houses squat randomly, as in a fistful of stones flung at a hillside of mud. There are no roads, just well-worn tracks threading the cottages.

Higher again, on a knoll above the rooftops, a military post, and inside a small fenced area a soldier stares across the gorge to a widening cleft, beyond which layers of green hillside peel back to the Macedonian border.

We were discovered by children first. Then a few stooped old men. Someone ran off for the doctor, a youngish man, clean-shaven, in a polo neck and an old blazer. He went off to find the chief of the village council. One man, pale and sweating from tilling the yard outside his cottage, put down a crude grubber and gazed at us with astonishment. The women, shy as forest creatures, hid in doorways.

We learned we were in an area known as the "black place": Gryke e Leze.

The name had stuck after the Serbs, in 1912, marched into the gorge and slaughtered 520 men and women. Pregnant women were butchered and left to die. The Serbs had got as far as a village which used to stand at the mouth of the gorge.

From the chief of the council, a small bowlegged man with a handsome grey moustache, Bill and I learned that we were the first foreigners in Topojani since the Serbs.

Thirty or forty faces were peering and grinning—all of

them stunted and malnourished. Boys of twelve and thirteen stood no taller than my waist.

The doctor said they were suffering from dystrophy and malnutrition, while the adults had to contend with chronic bronchitis and rheumatism.

"He has a clinic but no medicine," said Anila.

The chief told Bill that the village had learnt as recently as a month ago that grain supplies had arrived in Albania from abroad. But he added it would be another ten or twenty years before such aid would arrive in Topojani.

"We believe we eat," he said. "In fact, we eat potatoes because the soil cannot grow anything else. Topojani has always been poor."

"Always?"

"We have a very old woman who remembers the Serbs. She will tell you, all her life she has starved."

Topojani was out of macaroni, soap, salt. Before the regime collapsed they used to carry potatoes down the gorge to Kukës and barter for peppers and cheese and meat.

But there were other problems. Topojani had grown to an unsustainable size. The chief told Bill it had started out with just five houses.

"Oh? When was that?"

"Two hundred years ago," said the man.

The Ismshj family had fled a blood feud in Shkodër and made for this bolt-hole tucked away in the gorge of the farthermost corner of the country. Now there were fifteen families with the Ismshj name and the Topojani population stood at 1,150, spread over some three hundred houses.

The chief spoke of his concern about the winter. They had no bread. The few goats were without feed.

Bill listened but said nothing.

Last summer, the chief continued, many of them had walked into Kukës to sleep out in the fields under sheets of plastic. "If you ask a ninety-year-old woman or a child, they will say the same thing: 'We don't want to live here. We have lost all hope.'"

One of the houses abandoned by a family for a plastic sheet in the fields outside Kukës has been turned into a coffeehouse. Eleven o'clock in the morning and it is smoky and dark. We feel our way like the blind for a table by the wall. As soon as candles are lit, the walls flare up with silhouettes of shaggy manes of hair. There are some thirty men sitting around, watchful and silent.

Bill says, "Go ahead. Ask after Shapallo."

I hadn't thought to ask Shapallo for the names of relatives. But thinking about it, I remembered he had been born in a different village. I guess he had been dropped into Topojani, the same way the doctor had: an outsider, city-trained, sent to run the clinic.

Anila speaks with the doctor, who passes on the question, and the chief of the village council then takes it up with the rest of the room.

Several times I hear Shapallo's name mentioned. But there are no takers.

"Anila, perhaps if you mention Shapallo was the dentist here?"

"Yes. I have said this already." Then she shushes me as a chair scrapes back on the floor. A shadow standing in the corner of the room recalls that Shapallo was transferred to another village.

"And his wife and children?"

"They went to join him some months afterwards."

"He had a clinic."

"Yes, it is where the doctor is now."

"That's it?"

"They don't remember Mister Shapallo," concludes Anila.

In a last-ditch effort I pass on everything that Shapallo has told me about his life here, as well as the other things he had told Munz, such as his teaching the village children gymnastics; on National Independence Day he used to construct elaborate pyramids using up to a dozen children, each one supporting another. But no one in the room remembers the pyramids of children. The dentist is recalled as a quiet man who kept to himself.

"He must have had some friends. Surely someone remembers something?"

"A tall man, yes?" But the council chief is just checking to reassure himself.

The shadow who remembers Shapallo's "transfer" says he knows where the family lived, if that is any help.

We wander along a track that climbs to the memorial recalling the 1912 massacre. From there we slide down a bank to a small cottage all on its own.

The yard has been tilled to grow potatoes. Chicken wire covers the windows, and there are bits of feather stuck in the wire. The cottage boasts two rooms. The floors of both are covered in a white cement of chicken shit and feathers.

The chief picks up the story here. He seems to remember now. It had been after the family's "transfer" that an official from Kukës arrived with six hens and roosters to start Topojani's poultry development.

Poultry had flourished for a time, but disease had cut their numbers and then a blizzard had wiped out all but a plucky rooster. For six months the council chief visited one village after another in search of a hen. There was talk among the younger men of slipping across the Macedonian border to steal a hen, but nothing came of it. In the morning the hotheads walked away from this talk and returned to peeling stones off the hillside to create another potato patch.

Shapallo was remembered as a footnote to the period that had succeeded his "transfer," when Topojani, for a brief time, had enjoyed eggs and fowl.

46

Shapallo eased himself onto his elbows. Anila rearranged the pillows behind him. He took a sip of coffee. Then Anila took the cup from him and Shapallo lay back to await our news.

I had been dreading this; all the way back down the gorge it had occurred to me to wonder what kind of "good news" Professor Kupi could possibly have taken back to King Leka and the Albanian communities living abroad.

"Mister Shapallo asks, Is Topojani still beautiful?"

"Yes," I said.

"Good." Shapallo smiled. "This is surely good. My house. Did they show it to you?"

"A lovely cottage."

Shapallo sighed. "But in spring . . ." In spring, he said, Topojani revealed its soul.

With an embarrassed smile he asked, coyly, "Did the people remember me, their old dentist?"

"Yes," I said, but Anila explained at much greater length and Shapallo was evidently pleased by what he heard. He smiled happily and his head nodded against his pillow.

Anila, my second witness, trained her black eyes on me and quietly explained, "I was telling Mister Shapallo that everyone had fond memories of him and his family. Everyone, without exception."

That night, in the room next to Shapallo's, I pulled the bedcovers around me and caught up with Zog in exile.

The lack of recognition caused him his greatest anxiety. Zog worked hard and spent prodigiously to bolster his image and legitimise his position as head of the Albanians. He created legations in Turkey and Egypt, a mission in Washington, and four consular posts. He created a shadow government with four or five Ministers. Increasingly desperate, he offered the Anglo-Jewish Association a Jewish settlement in Albania if the Jews would consent to his regaining the throne.

During the war the Royal Household passed through a succession of residences. There was the undignified scramble out of France just a few hours ahead of the Nazis' march into Paris. In London Zog installed the Royal Household in the Ritz off Piccadilly: of his thirty-four-strong entourage, six were listed as H.M. Ordinance Officers; these were Zog's bodyguards, Mati tribesmen whose sawn-off shotguns never left their sides. From the Ritz Zog moved the entourage to a villa in Sunningdale near Ascot. Soon after, there was another move, to Henley, where it was left to Queen Geraldine to get out the gardening tools and cultivate a large garden to feed the entourage. Zog would not permit the men in his entourage to do any work—after all, he argued, they have given up everything to be with him; so it was left to Geraldine to do the gardening and the cooking, and to clean out the chicken coop.

Following Zog's death Geraldine faced problems of a different kind: the main one what to do with a six-foot-eight princeling. He was without employable skills and a royal household is nothing without funds.

The years tick by. Geraldine quietly sells one piece of jewellery after another in order to keep up appearances. Following King Leka's coronation the Krupps in Hamburg offer to take on the new King as an apprentice arms dealer. But the pay is meagre and acceptance of the position would require the Royal Household to move to Hamburg.

The problems of a job, money, expense accounts remain until Leka turns to his father's friends. Prince Faisal, for one, introduces Leka to leading Saudi businessmen.

All is well for a while. There is money coming in and Leka is generally well received in the Middle East. There are motorcades. Escorts. Guards snap to attention. Flags are raised over hotels. The curtains pulled on all the windows on the floor of whatever hotel he happens to be staying at.

But the frustrations which go with the job of royalty in exile are beginning to mount. For example, he has a uniform but no regiment. He has guns but no target. He is forever training, and training others for the beachhead landing to honour his father's deathbed hallucination. There are other times when Leka is simply the wayward son in search of war.

He has been gone some months on one of his trips to the Middle East when Geraldine is visited by an ambassador bearing a message from the Saudi King voicing disapproval of King Leka's training for the Yemen war. Leka has been making a nuisance of himself, disturbing other hotel guests and running around the hotel at four o'clock in the morning in full military kit.

The ambassador tactfully explains the impracticalities of the King involving himself in guerrilla warfare. He is too tall for a start—"and there is no way we could protect your giant son."

Leka returns to Spain, where he continues his hand-grenade practice and small-arms training.

Geraldine would appear to be comparatively well adjusted. She manages to cut a royal figure on the embassy cocktail circuit in Madrid, but obviously the Queen has given some thought to vocational guidance. She speaks of eventually returning to Albania "newly trained" as a professional in modern health administration.

Meanwhile, the lives of King Zog's sisters, the Princesses, fade away in the curtained gloom of a Cannes apartment. Only occasionally do they get to see the light of day, and then only during trips to the casino in Monte Carlo.

Two of the Princesses die on the same night—a third goes less than a week later. Perhaps this is their finest hour as they are driven in a hearse to Paris, followed all the way by a car draped in flowers "tied with scarlet and black ribbons." At Thiais, buses have ferried in grieving Albanians from exile communities all over Europe—"The only sound in the heavy cemetery air was their calling the names of Queen Geraldine and King Leka, over and over again."

It is during the seventies that King Leka manages to recover some of the royal family's former prosperity after an offer from the Shah of Iran to set up his "young cousin" in business. For the next few years Leka supplies mobile cranes for the Ports and Shipping Authority of Iran. With these spoils he is able to replace the pawned court jewellery. He presents his mother with a new crown and a set of tiaras in sapphires and diamonds.

In exile other traditions are upheld. Consent from various leaders of exile communities scattered worldwide is sought by the King to marry Susan of Sydney. In the absence of a traditional wedding gown, Susan's Sydney dressmaker copies one from an old encyclopaedia photograph. On the day, the King disports himself in the uniform of colonel of the Royal Albanian Guards with the Order of Skanderbeg, a military decoration first introduced by his father. In attendance at the wedding are other royal exiles: Queen Farida of Egypt, King Simeon and Queen Margarita of Bulgaria, a clutch of princesses. Cables from around the world are read out to the wedding guests, among them a message from Queen Elizabeth II. Guests recall the tall King slicing the wedding cake with his sword.

For the rest of the seventies, through to the early eighties, it is business as usual. Leka pops up in Thai border camps to cadge operational and communications equipment for his Free Albania units.

Queen Geraldine visits the exile communities in New York and Peterborough, in Canada. She goes to Washington and is received at the Capitol by senators who whisk her off for lunch. The Queen remembers them as being "charming, cultivated men, but they did not know one thing about Albania."

Queen Geraldine and her giant son have become relics whom no one knows what to do with. The matters of sentimental attachment, the fight for shelf space, have to be juggled with a changing order of things. It is left to Leka's former playmate, Prince Juan Carlos, to prevail on the royal family to leave Spain. Leka's combat training has become intolerable, and besides, there are new political sensitivities. Franco is ill, and Spain teeters on the threshold of entering the new Europe.

Geraldine goes off to live with her sister, the Princess Apponyi, and whiles away her time reading romantic novels. Barbara Cartland is a favourite.

King Leka and Queen Susan are shunted about various African countries before a haven is found in South Africa. And here, too, royalty seeks out its own. King Leka and Queen Susan are guests of the King of Zululand.

It is in South Africa that the King accomplishes his finest political act in his and Susan's conceiving a son named Anwar (after President Sadat) Zog Baudouin (after the King of Belgium) Reza (after the Shah).

It is left to a proud granny to remind us that "Albania had a Crown Prince and the Zogu dynasty was assured."

47

Back in Tirana, Munz rang from the hotel. Kadris said he would meet Shapallo off the train. He seemed to think that Mister Gina would make the Democrats' car available for the run out to Savra. And so we said goodbye to Shapallo. He showed no disappointment to be heading back to Savra. His memories of Topojani remained intact. In that sense he hadn't risked losing that final thing he could believe in—a home.

In the morning we saw him off. Then we walked back to the Dajti, where Diani was waiting to ring Nexhmije.

She rang the telephone number which Illir had scribbled down, and Nexhmije answered—which was to be expected, of course. But for Diani, Nexhmije belonged to the old pantheon of saints. Nexhmije had shared the royal podium. It was scarcely believable that she should answer her own telephone and ask that we avoid the back entrance.

"She did stress the 'front entrance,' " said Diani.

Five o'clock, and although it was dark I could see no sign of security.

Nexhmije came to the door herself, a woman with long grey hair tied back in a schoolmistress bun. We shook hands and followed her up the stairs to the first-floor apartment.

Inside the door we were shown into an austere living room. On one wall, a large colour portrait of Enver and herself standing outside their holiday home in Vlorë, one year before the Emperor's death. Two bowls of plastic flowers stood on a coffee table. Another wall was taken up with bookshelves, but few books.

I had thought to ask after Enver's real library, but any possibility of this becoming a question-and-answer session was quickly dispelled by Nexhmije. She wanted to talk about old times, and to this end she had prepared a speech.

We hear about Albania's isolation, and how the country's drift towards China had come about after its abandonment by the West.

"Abandonment by the West?"

In a strong, disapproving voice, she says, "Please let me conclude."

Nexhmije continues—she continued, uninterrupted, for two hours.

It is a lengthy dissertation scrambled by Diani's increasingly panicked translation to the point of incoherence. On she goes—out of control, and meeting my glances with petrified eyes that beg me not to ask what it is Nexhmije has just said.

And Nexhmije, none the wiser, presses on with her "howevers" and "buts" and "wherefores," and in this way the entire postwar history of Albania is bridged.

I am scribbling down nonsense when the monologue suddenly terminates, and when I look up there is Nexhmije, composed and happy as a cat.

"Did I talk too long?" she asks. "I hope not."

"Noooo," replies Diani, her hands pressed to her knees, like a child wanting to please.

"Good." The cat smiles.

She excuses herself then, and returns with a tray of coffee and raki.

She is pleased, very pleased, to have the opportunity to speak with friends. It occurs to me that she is, of course, referring to Cliff's letter.

"These days," she says, "I find myself in need of friends."

We talk about television, her favourite programmes. She doesn't care for Yugoslav television. It shows too many American programmes. She prefers RAI for its sober political discussions.

Nexhmije is in the middle of explaining an invitation she received to appear on a French show when a power cut pitches the room into darkness. Nexhmije, however, is ready for this. We both are, and Nexhmije reaches for a penlight the moment I flick on Bill's torch. Our beams cross over the top of the coffee table and we laugh about that.

Nexhmije finds a candle from the sideboard. I hold the torch while she gets the candle lit, then she takes care to move the candle closer to where I have been sitting so that I can see my notes better.

This is not going the way I had wished. I note her frail ankles, the tidy composition of her hands. Nexhmije looks like somebody's grandmother.

Does she have nightmares? Did she see the way the Ceausescus died—the unceremonious way Nicolae and Elena were backed up to a wall, the way they sagged to their knees like two sacks? These are the questions the victims of bad biografi had asked in Rruga Ndre Mjeda.

In October from a window in the Dajti Bill had watched

a crowd of 50,000 swarm up the Boulevard of Martyrs intent on violence, chanting, "Death to the widow!"

I quietly let Diani know that I would like to hear about Nexhmije's dreams at night. What enters her head at four o'clock in the morning these days?

A look of terror comes into Diani's eyes, and a slightly different question is asked.

Nexhmije, she says, is concerned for the young people. She worries about them. They have been a little spoilt, she feels.

"As far as the economic and psychological changes are concerned, I am a little pessimistic," she says.

The young people have not realised how hard people in the West work. She doubts whether the youth are equipped with the right attitude to cope.

"Perhaps we are to blame, like parents who keep their children indoors. Now the children want to go out and away from the family."

She manages, somehow with a straight face, to explain why Albania had locked up its borders for so long.

"We had not the possibility to allow people to go abroad because they did not have the funds."

Of Albania's isolationist path: this is the fault of the West. Where was the support from the West after her husband's criticism of Khrushchev and the country's split with the Soviet Union in the early sixties?

"Not even Italy came to our aid."

Long before Dubcek, before Lech Walesa, Comrade Enver had attacked Soviet imperialism. And what happened? she asked. China had been the only one to hold out a hand.

Then had come the split with China, and ever since, Albania had been left to live off its reserves.

We leave, with Nexhmije waving us goodbye from her door. On the street, though, we glance back to a curious sight. The power is on in the apartments above and below Nexhmije's. I am left with the rueful thought that perhaps halfway up that dim stairwell Nexhmije is thinking how well the interview went for her. She even agreed to a second visit.

Diani is ecstatic. "Did you see? She kissed me at the door!"

She makes a thing of flicking the kiss from her cheek. She agrees that her father will be very pleased.

Her father is an old partisan who spends his days in striped pyjamas prostrate before a television set. I had met him earlier in the day, and he had rolled off the bed and walked timorously over to a chest of drawers to get his old French pistol.

In her high piping voice Diani said, "My father wishes to tell you that this is the pistol he used in the War of Liberation."

I turned the pistol round with elaborate care, and the old partisan received my compliments with an impatient nod of his head. He took the pistol back and plodded off to the drawer, where he wrapped it in cloth; the party trick over, he fell back on his bed and grinned up at the Albanian folk music playing on the television. He would be very proud that his daughter had had an audience with Nexhmije.

48

Two days later, Nexhmije was arrested. The newspapers reported with some glee that she had been taken by surprise.

She had been about to enter the car which, each day, took her to the hearing into the alleged abuses of the former block men, when instead she was shown to another car.

"Her wrists were embellished with bracelets she had never dreamt of . . ." cheered the *Sindikalist* newspaper.

Several days passed before we caught up with Illir. This time around he was more talkative.

We bumped into him outside his gate. He invited us up for coffee. Inside the door of Nexhmije's apartment he tossed off his coat and pulled off his gloves like a man home from the office. He was spirited and worked up by what had happened.

Animated in that way of bush lawyers sure of their points, Illir began to cite the Helsinki Agreement in his mother's defence. This was the same agreement to which his father's regime had refused to be a signatory. Nexhmije, he argued, posed neither a threat to society nor an obstruction to the gathering of evidence. By the terms of the Helsinki Agreement she should not be in prison.

There were other problems. Nexhmije was having difficulties obtaining the services of a lawyer—another delicious irony. One lawyer who had represented Nexhmije in seven hearings had suddenly abandoned her without a word.

Another lawyer had taken up her case only to inexplicably drop it. Nexhmije had tried to reach him, but he refused to take her calls. Still another lawyer had withdrawn because of threats.

In one of the hearings it had come down to Illir to represent his mother. That particular battle had been small beer. In May the previous year, Nexhmije had left the grand residence in the block for these six rooms above the customs house. But this apartment as well, the prosecutor had claimed, was unjustifiably spacious for just one person. So wily Illir had moved in with his wife and children.

At that stage the scoreboard read: Nexhmije 1, the prosecutor's office 0.

Now Nexhmije was in a small cell in the prison near the railway station. The cell was without a glass pane in its window, and without heat. Illir had visited with her only once, and that was to bring his mother fresh clothing and some French novels.

We sat in the same living room with Illir as we had with Nexhmije, and this time Diani's translations were more collected.

"Illir's mother," she said, "had anticipated anything—even worse than prison."

"Worse?"

"She had feared something from a street mob. She has no fear for herself but for her grandchildren."

"Of course."

"She is convinced that her trial will have nothing to do with the charges, that it will be a political one," added Illir. "My mother believes she will be the sacrificial lamb."

49

It was drawing close to Christmas now, although in downtown Tirana you wouldn't have known it. The power cuts continued as more and more electric appliances were brought across the border, overloading Albania's light-bulb electricity supply.

Thugs fought their way to the front of bread shops and sold loaves at a markup to those at the back, more often than not the elderly and infirm.

One morning Bill came down to breakfast with a long face. He had just heard from Kukës. The warehouse we had visited with Mustaph had been looted and set afire. A ten-year-old boy and a policeman had been killed.

The trees between Tirana and Durrës had been chopped down to the ground, and there was talk of another boat exodus.

It was time to look up Enver's place of exile, and on the outskirts of Tirana, with Diani, I found the former Emperor undergoing "rehabilitation." Inside a foundry warehouse, a statue of Enver was lying ill-temperedly, face and toes pointed in the same direction, a Napoleonic hand thrust behind his back. Alongside stood Lenin; his arms had been torn off. *Dulla* had been scrawled on another bust of Enver in support of the rumours that Enver had been gay in his youth.

And here was the prized find. In a small reserved area lay remnants of the magnificent block of marble from which

Kristaq Rama had sculpted his pharaoh. The foundry fore-man said the "new" sculptors drop by and take what they need—and in this way the pharaoh has found himself re-created into ashtrays, lampstands, and small gift-sized elephants.

The new heroes were parked around the side of the warehouse. These were scaled-down busts of writers and poets who had led the Albanian renaissance during the Ottoman rule. Their bright new white alabaster surfaces had been left out to dry in the sun. Over their shoulders, across the railway line, the grey smudge dripping from the wintry branches belonged to the ugly housing blocks with their slit windows and cramped balconies stuffed with washing.

On my last Sunday in Tirana I did something that would have pleased Nick. I attended a church service in one of the classrooms of the University Publishing House. The congregation dribbled through the doors in their bright-coloured plastics and scarves. They shook out their umbrellas in the gloom of the foyer, where the light bulbs had long since expired, and where Diani's friends, the German apostles, waited in their dark suits to direct the traffic by torch into the classroom.

People shuffled into place behind the trestled tables. Outside, a boy held a stick insect up to a broken window, and it started to rain. An older man in the next row dabbed his forehead with a handkerchief. As his discomfort mounted, a medical student took his pulse and nodded that he was fine for the moment. But the man went on wincing; then the pain would pass, and from behind I could see the bright, laughing blue of his eyes as he peered through the folds of his handkerchief at the young German pastor promising eternity and peace in heaven. Beside him his granddaughter sat on a bench and peeled a hard-boiled egg.

The congregation stood to sing and I found it surprisingly moving—to be in a classroom with ordinary folk whose simple hope was for something better than what they had known.

Diani had shopped around. She had tried the Lutherans and the Catholics. She liked the apostles because they provided medicine and sweets to every child they baptised. She didn't care for the American evangelical style which we had watched together on television, a crowd worked up to a fever at the Tirana soccer stadium during the summer.

"Jesus is with us here, tonight. Can you say 'Jesus?'"

Twenty-five thousand voices obediently roared back.

"Let's hear that again. Jesus! Jesus! Jesus! Let's all say, 'Jesus is the Lord!' Let's say, 'Jesus is the King of Albania!'"

Later, in the foyer, I met the apostles, Wilfred and Helmut; they poured scorn on the Americans.

"They came through here—filled the stadium, put on a big show, and left town," said Wilfred. "We've been here six months. But we're not here to hand out gifts and parcels. Their souls are the important thing."

Diani skipped away from the publishing house, gaily ignoring the rain and laughing aloud at the joke of Helmut's name, which in Albanian translated to "poison" and "shit."

I caught up with her to say goodbye. It was impossible to thank her enough. I pressed an envelope of American notes into her hand and she ran off up the street crying.

A final night out with Bill at the Petronella, a new private-enterprise restaurant tucked away at the end of an alley off the Boulevard of Martyrs, ended with us both drinking too much Bulgarian red wine. He told me Albania was his "last duty." A desk job in Washington awaited him on his return. Sharon? She does exist. Bill popped a photograph onto the table of an attractive woman in her early forties. Sharon was rolling a pebble back and forth under her sneaker while she smiled at the camera. In the Petronella, Bill, glass in hand, smiled back, pissy-eyed.

A final visit to Fatos and Brikena, and afterwards a look in the door of the Naim Frasheri bookshop on the ground floor. On every shelf were newly translated copies of Webster's American Biographies, on "three thousand significant American lives."

50

In the morning I climbed into a red taxi. Munz lowered his head in the window to make sure I had everything. Bags. Coat. Scarf. Passport. I had to unwrap Nick's mother's cake before he would believe that someone was actually taking food out of Albania.

"To Italy of all places!" He laughed. He was happy; he was going home soon.

Outside Tirana we slowed down due to some broken glass and I happened to look out at the right time to catch Mentor's Volvo, his neighbour asleep in the back, a pair of socked feet sticking up on the headrest of the front passenger seat.

In Durrës there was time to take the road winding up the hill from the old town to King Zog's palace. As we drew up to a courtyard, a soldier with bad acne and a mouthful of food rushed out, waving his arms to block our way.

I wound down the window and pointed to Zog's palace.

"Is not Zog's palace. Is President Ramiz's summer house."

"Ramiz. Ramiz," said the driver tiredly.

From a vantage point beneath Zog's palace, or Ramiz's summer house, Illir Ikonomi, along with a Durrës friend and a Finnish journalist, had watched the frantic mobs swarm up and down the wharf in search of a ship to board. Rumour had turned them from one end of the wharf to the other, like lemmings.

Illir had told me about it in Tirana, how his friend had suddenly upped and left them on the hill to join the scene down on the wharves.

"My friend had always wanted to travel," Illir said. "He often spoke of the foreign places he dreamt of visiting."

Later in the day, Illir had gone to the man's family home to break to the parents the news that their son had boarded a ship for Italy. He hadn't yet started to explain when the son turned up at the door with the full story.

On boarding the ship Illir's friend had been asked his occupation. Everyone had voiced relief when he said, "Engineer."

"What luck," they said. "We're looking for an engineer."

He had tried to explain what he had meant by engineer, that he was a mechanical engineer—not a ship's engineer. But nobody wanted to hear this and he had been led down to the navigator's room—just to see what he could do to make the ship move.

Everyone aboard was getting nervous. They were anxious for the ship to depart before the situation changed. The mechanical engineer, aware of the urgency and against his better judgement, pressed a button and the ship began to move at a much faster speed than it should have, and minutes later the nose of the ship had struck the sea wall at the port opening.

There the ship stranded itself. Some of the would-be refugees had lowered themselves on ropes down the side and run along the sea wall, hopping from boulder to boulder. Others, too shocked to move, had sat down on deck and wept.

51

A large crowd had already gathered. The policeman checking passengers through leaned backwards against the tide of people. He saw my passport and nodded. I squeezed through and ran across no-man's-land for the customs house, where other passengers had gathered with their luggage.

Here the minutes ticked away. A soldier at another gate kept directing us back to wait in line at the side of the customs building. The ship was due to leave in another thirty minutes. None of us knew what was required, or how to go about boarding the ship. Occasionally the door to the customs house would open and an official would come out to smoke a cigarette in the cold sunshine. I tried the door half a dozen times, but the officials always bolted it after themselves.

One of the passengers, an impatient older man in a grey suit, suddenly rallied his family. They picked up their suitcases and I followed them around the side of the customs building. About a hundred metres up ahead were the rest of the passengers. They had been herded together about fifty metres from the ship.

In small groups we were grudgingly let through. It was never clear when to go; it was a case of waiting until the backs of the soldiers were turned and sprinting for the hold. Or quite impulsively, four or five passengers would suddenly make a dash, and the soldiers would rush to that end of the crowd to prevent more passengers following suit. They raised their batons and the untidy fringes of the crowd fell back.

In the hold of the ship I joined another line. But there was less frenzy here. The passengers relaxed and the line moved forward in a civilised fashion. At last, at the bottom of the steps, I presented my ticket for Bari. In the lounge I joined another line to hand in my passport at the purser's office for "reasons of security."

Out on the deck I found a seat in the sun. The ship was still tied to the wharf, but everyone aboard had slipped into a different gear. They paused at entranceways to allow others through. They closed their eyes and basked in the sun. Further along the rail I saw the prostitute from the Dajti. She was in the same fur coat, but she had new company. A large fleshy-faced Dane was eating a sandwich, while his older companion cut up an orange. The woman wore sunglasses and she crossed her legs, and when offered a segment of orange she put it in her mouth but did not chew; she took the orange like a pill.

The ship was still tied up at the wharf but to all intents and purposes we had left Albania, and for some reason I felt compelled to write down the date in my notebook.

I had reached the point where Swire, fifty years ago, ends his book—standing on the stern of the Lussino and watching its wake trail back towards Durrës. He closes his account in a most wonderful way: "I went to the saloon to write the last page of my Albanian diary. When I had laid down my pen the fresh breeze caught and turned the written page. My Albania days were done." But I still had unfinished business to attend to. I picked up Nick's mother's cake and my bag and found a table next to a window in the lounge.

There was a jolt as we parted from the wharf. The grille on the bar went up. Stainless-steel lids were noisily lifted off pans of paprika chicken, fresh lasagna, pasta, salads, and golden chips. The next time I looked up, away to the port side, the Albanian coastline had melted into the mountains.

I tried to imagine the same moment aboard the freighters during the "boat exodus." Albania sinking into the distance, and up on deck, in hot, cramped conditions, the Albanians with their crazy notions as to what lay ahead, pieced together from hearsay and wild speculation.

I thought of Nick's map of the North Yorkshire moors, his poaching another's journey, the way he'd boned up on Sherlock Holmes for additional information on the moors, until eventually he had been able to imagine the landscape the dotted line passed through.

Performing a similar role, Cliff's shortwave radio had helped to rein in the outside world.

My imaginative reach had been given an additional boost by Martinborough's founder, John Martin, who had named the streets after all his favourite places visited around the world. Kansas Street was the outer street on a grid designed after the British Union Jack, with streets named after New York, Rio, Genoa, Durban, Dublin, Strasbourg, and Ohio.

For a time it had been a New Year's tradition to hold street parties, and Genoa's was always the most popular. The few people in Kansas who could be bothered dressing up in cowboy or hayseed outfits invariably ended way over in Genoa for pizza and beer before the night was done. There was accordion music and what people in those days described as "gaiety."

For some reason people stayed up later in Genoa and were still dancing and falling into each other's arms long after the blinds had been drawn in Durban and Cardiff. Genoa had a reputation of being the "colourful side of town."

My uncle's wife, Louise, was an angry woman. She liked to dress in black—stockings, skirt, and blouse—and apply lashings of red lipstick.

"You're looking luscious tonight, Louise," my uncle would say admiringly. From the couch he'd add, "I'll wait up for you."

"Don't," she always said.

Louise and Frank Latta one New Year's sang love duets and danced up one side of Genoa and down the other.

Around dawn a farmer five kilometres outside town saw Frank and Louise walking back home past the paddocks and the cows and sheep. Louise had mistaken Frank for somebody else. Dawn broke pale and emptily over the southern Wairarapa and suddenly she realised that she was running off with a plasterer. It was Frank. Frank Latta. And Frank had also come to his senses. He had a cricket match on for that afternoon. The annual town-and-country fixture.

Louise had turned up Kansas carrying her black shoes and picking her way home across the front lawns as the sun hit the corrugated iron roofs.

She was gone inside a year. Louise could take Kansas no longer. She wanted to rejoin the world, she said. My uncle, under the impression Louise was staying with friends further up the line in Dannevirke, received a letter from Melbourne, Australia.

He continued to keep the photograph of Louise pruning the roses in the front garden on his bedside table. He felt Louise just needed to get something out of her system and she'd be back soon enough.

I kept coming over the hill for another two summers, although the New Year's Eve street-party tradition ended after Louise's departure. People saw the unhappy face of my uncle about town and you could see their thoughts shift back to the previous New Year's Eve and the imaginative risk Frank, the plasterer, and Louise had brought to Genoa.

52

On the midnight train to Rome I fell asleep with the taste of a fresh ham sandwich in my mouth. In the morning I strode lightly from a station platform. Outside the Termini the commuters dispersed. There was an appealing order, and the surfaces of the city were clean. In the bistros beneath glass counters the pastries and eclairs were displayed like jewellery. For the next few days, however, I was to come across pockets of Albania.

The Franciscan monastery was colder than I remembered, and Nick more sallow and creepy.

He rang the number Leila had written down and spoke with the manager of a restaurant in Carsoli. The manager said to ring back in twenty minutes—it was the lunch hour and Fatmir was behind with the dishes.

For the time being we sat in the Franciscan telephone room, a cold cell on the ground floor. The telephone was one of Nick's responsibilities. He was expected to keep tabs on toll calls. A tatty old exercise book hung by a string from a nail.

I remembered his mother's cake and reached into my bag. Nick grinned, nodded. He looked at it for all of five seconds and threw it on a shelf with a pile of ecclesiastical magazines.

He was more interested to find out whom I had met in Shkodër. Professor Pepa and Gjyzepina drew no reaction. But his face coloured at the mention of Mimi and Illir.

He glanced away with embarrassment.

"Illir is nothing," he said.

He wanted to know why I hadn't contacted the priests —the ones who could really speak of suffering.

I mentioned Nexhmije and Nick's eyes blazed with indignation.

"You did not speak to the right people. These are terrible, terrible people."

He couldn't contain himself. He got up and walked about shaking his head.

The next time he tried the restaurant, he got through to Fatmir and a time and rendezvous were agreed to.

The brigadier hadn't given me a telephone number for his son, Eloni, just an address. Caprarola was a good hour-and-a-half drive from Rome; getting there would take the best part of a morning on a bus. Nick said he couldn't spare the time. It was impossible. He had to be back by midday to feed the friars. There were other problems besides. I think my knowledge of Nick's background had altered everything. Nick seemed less heroic, and perhaps in his eyes I had become less trustworthy. Anyway, his excuses veered off into unintelligibility, and when we shook hands it was with the knowledge that we were parting company for the final time.

The solution was left as to where I was renting a room. The landlady's son put me in touch with his former girlfriend, Emanuella, and one fine Sunday morning we followed via Cassia out of the city into the countryside.

Greenpeace stickers plastered Emanuella's car, inside and out. Stickers demanding animal rights; stickers of endangered species, pandas, whales, elephants, and a weird shovel-beaked bird which I had thought to be already extinct. An anti-vivisectionist organisation had the dashboard.

I had warned her that this trip out to Caprarola was a long shot. The person we were driving to meet didn't know we were coming.

"That's okay," she said. "I wasn't doing anything."

It was a brilliantly fine day, and shortly before Viterbo we turned off the motorway onto a country road. Emanuella slowed and we wound down the windows.

"New Zealand," she suddenly said. "I would like to go there."

"Why?"

"Because it is so far away."

Emanuella's was a sad story. Her mother had leapt from an apartment building when Emanuella was two. When she was old enough she had learnt of her mother's severe postnatal depression, and she had never quite cured herself of the idea that she had had some responsibility for her mother's death.

At the age of twelve, Emanuella, her brother, and her father had moved to a bigger house. The last room to be packed up was her father's study. He told her not to touch the desk, that he would clear out his drawers.

The telephone rang and her father was called out on an errand. While he was gone Emanuella went through his desk and found a warrant for her father's arrest, a charge sheet, and other papers exonerating him for any part in her mother's death.

She left everything the way she had found it, and rather than challenge her father, who was a strict and domineering figure, Emanuella had lived with her secret. She was twelve years old and completely dependent on the man she now believed had driven, if not pushed, her mother to her death.

She had spent her teenage years dreaming and thinking ahead to when she would leave school and escape the house. But she had gone on to university and her dependency had continued—even after she had graduated, since she couldn't find a job. She had recently moved into her own apartment, paid for by her father.

"How much to fly to New Zealand?" she asked.

Caprarola sprang up on both sides of the road—a long, unbroken line of small, clannish buildings, and via Filipo Nikolai climbed to a huge cathedral at the top of the rise.

We parked by a sweets stall and found Eloni's address, a building undergoing renovation. We ducked under scaffolding and climbed five flights of stairs cut from stone. Plasterer's dust hung in the air.

On the top floor an old woman came to the door. I heard Emanuella ask after the Albanos and the woman showed us out to a balcony off the landing. The back side of via Filipo Nikolai fell away to a deep green valley; the drop was sheer and breathtaking.

Eloni's door was partially open. We pushed through and two men looked up from watching soccer on television.

"Eloni?"

A slim man dressed like a waiter in dark slacks and a white shirt smiled pleasantly.

Emanuella explained whom we were after, and the man in a white singlet pointed to each of the five beds pressed together in the small room, and said, "Albano, Albano, Albano, Albano, Albano."

"Eloni Idrizllari?"

The man in the dark slacks smiled to indicate that we had arrived in the right place. He came to the door and we shook hands; then he picked up his jacket and closed the door after him.

On the stairs Emanuella explained that our waiter was not Eloni.

"However," she said, "he knows where Eloni is and he'll take us there now."

Besnik called Eloni from a café to tell him he had a visitor from Savra.

It was a further ten minutes' drive winding down through the valley we had seen from the balcony outside the Albanians' room, to Lake Bella Venere, a weekend resort. We drew up to a small grey lake, and Eloni, with the same nimble build as the brigadier, walked out of his father's shadow in blue jeans and a denim jacket with Bruce Springsteen blaring from the bar over his shoulder.

He had been expecting me, he said. Paitim had sent a telegram.

Eloni was one of half a dozen Albanians employed to look after the maintenance of the resort. It was the off-season and the Albanians were plainly enjoying having the place to themselves. We walked over to the bar and sat outside at a table without an umbrella. There was a lovely view of the lake. It was raked with shadows from trees that had lost their leaves.

In the absence of raki Eloni shouted for coffee and beer, and one of his compatriots leapt behind the bar.

Eloni was eager for news from Savra. He leant over his

beer and asked after the brigadier's current state of mind. "Is he angry? What did he say about me?"

Eloni spoke "TV Italian" and he had to concentrate to understand Emanuella's quick explanation that his father was very pleased that he was in Italy. He slowly computed that and threw back his arms.

"Ah! That is because I have work. That's all he ever speaks of. Work. Work. Work."

The brigadier had always been onto him to work harder. Eloni had been kicked out of school for smoking. He had worked in the fields for a few months but had hated it, and had given it up to help the brigadier at home, until the police threatened him with jail unless he worked.

In Italy he worked at two jobs, here at the resort and during the week helping to restore the building the Albanians were living in.

At the time of the news coming out of Durrës he was planning to walk to Greece. Instead, within half an hour of hearing about the rush on the boats, he joined the mobs walking into Lushnje to catch the train. They had jumped together, 90 percent of the passengers, he said, hanging from the bars and leaping for the tracks where the train slowed down to make the hairpin run inland, towards Tirana. They had run in a group, keeping their heads low. Police fired off shots overhead. A better reception awaited him at the wharves. Soldiers were protecting certain ships and pointing to others, waving them on and wishing them well. "Have a good trip," they said.

The *Panama* was the only ship left, and 6,000 had scrambled aboard the cement freighter. They sat in the hold;

through the night they huddled there and didn't set sail until dawn. As they entered open water there had been no cheering. Everyone was afraid of having been tricked. The *sigourimi* were rumoured to be aboard, and as the homeland dropped below the horizon, rumours had started up that Italy was no longer the destination. The ship was headed to India or Africa. The hours had ticked by without sight of the coastline.

At five o'clock Eloni said he saw a seagull. Then it grew dark and Italy rose out of the sea in a long line of lights. At midnight the cement freighter had dropped anchor at Brindisi. The Italians had given them the choice of staying on board or coming ashore.

"I was afraid we would be sent back," Eloni said. "So I came ashore, and for three nights we had slept by fires on the wharf."

He had just turned twenty and I couldn't help but think he was lucky that things had happened for him when they did; lucky that he had come of age when things were starting to fall apart. He'd acted on impulse without ever having dreamt of it first, and I admired him for having taken his opportunity so well.

He dropped his mouth over the top of the beer bottle, and I watched his face redden as Emanuella asked if he had run across the Ago brothers.

He came up for air with troubled eyes. "Who are the Ago brothers?"

"You don't know the Agos?"

He shook his head. So I explained about their coming from Savra. "They were also aboard the *Panama*."

He shook his head again and looked around for his compatriots, but they had all floated off with buckets and mops.

I described to him Leila's building, but he pretended not to recognise the place.

I wrote out the names of the Ago brothers on a piece of paper. Eloni took it and stared at it, shaking his head.

"But they are from Savra, yes. Here in Rome?"

He asked me to write down the telephone number of the Ago brothers and I did so, feeling sure that he would crumple the piece of paper as soon as we left.

53

The Ago brothers were waiting on the platform at Carsoli, a small alpine town framed by snow-capped peaks and dark green pines forty minutes' train ride from the Termini. With them was a large Italian, Giuseppe, and friends of his, two women in rather ugly fur coats who had driven up from Rome to practise their English.

The brothers had sorted it out amongst themselves in advance that Eduart would do the talking. We moved to the station café, where it was established that no one wanted a drink, then on to the waiting room, where we pulled two long benches together and sat down to talk.

It was a warm day, but their faces had the unhealthy, blemished colouring that often comes with prolonged exposure to raw cold. The eyes of the Ago brothers spoke of disappointment.

There had been nowhere to sit on the *Panama*, Eduart said. Apart from a cup of milk, they hadn't eaten since four o'clock the previous afternoon. Because they lacked the confidence to take a train they had walked from Savra across farmland and through the olive groves on the hills to avoid police checkpoints, all the way to Durrës, where they arrived at two in the morning and quietly boarded the cement freighter and lowered themselves into the hold. They were too excited to worry about food. They couldn't believe it was happening: all around them, tears of happiness and talk of what awaited them on the other side of the sea—the material goodies, the things they had seen on TV, the cars, a house, a job. They had talked amongst themselves about their favourite TV programmes. Their first view of Italy had seemed nothing less than miraculous.

But what had changed since then? There had been a string of refugee camps. And where previously they had watched Italian TV in Albania, now they watched it in Italy. America had replaced Italy as their El Dorado. In America, where their grandfather had gone, surely everything would come right.

They remembered Eloni on the wharves. Markelian especially. Leila's youngest son was angry that the Communists had received equal treatment from the Italians. He had expected the Communists to be thrown into jail. He was angry and disappointed to find that here in Italy biografi counted for nothing.

Markelian had questions of his own—he wanted to know my reason for having spoken with the brigadier. What was behind my meeting with Eloni's family?

I assured Markelian that there had been nothing other than curiosity before my meeting the brigadier.

He mulled that over; then he asked, What did the brigadier think of his son escaping to Italy?

"He was crushed," I said, and they were cheered to hear this. Markelian got up and punched the wall happily.

Then Eduart, with tears in his eyes, asked after his mother. On the telephone she sounds cold, he said. How had she seemed to me? Did she express a wish to go to America?

I didn't know the answer to that one. I wasn't sure what they wanted to hear. It was like being back in Savra. The chill cold of the waiting room and its sullen occupants. Italy had done nothing for them. They had no jobs other than Fatmir's dishwashing job at the restaurant. On RAI none of the commercials had mentioned unemployment. All they had succeeded in was bringing Savra's hopelessness with them—they had been caught out, and all the blind corners of Savra had resurfaced. They showed no signs of knowing how to overcome it; their final failure was this seeming inability to re-create themselves. In that sense, they had only partially completed the journey.

It all ended rather strangely in the square of Carsoli, outside a touristy pizza parlour, with the brothers requesting a photograph to send back to Leila of themselves raising the Fascist salute.

Their grandfather, Eduart proudly explained, had collaborated with the Nazis. More to the point, given their deep distrust of the Communists, anything the Communists opposed must automatically be a force for good.

The Ago brothers were not Fascists—just ignorant of the judgements the world had passed on Fascism. Forty-five years later, in this pretty alpine town outside Rome, I tried to explain to three young men why the photograph could not be taken.

54

For now I didn't know what to say or even how to begin a letter to Leila. But in the Honolulu airport I found something to send back to the old brigadier. A post-card of a very pretty Hawaiian girl with a lovely tanned hip and a big smile above a lei of frangipani. On the back, in "TV Italian," I jotted down Eloni's news for the brigadier. He was working!

Shapallo I sent a postcard of an old-fashioned surfer on a Malibu board coasting in on a small Waikiki wave. His arms spread wide and joined by a big smile of white teeth: the surfer's balance, at least for the moment, was perfectly assured.

I had a postcard for Cliff, too, of the Emperor carved from the twenty-five-tonne block of marble, and a few days later, back in New Zealand, I drove over the hill to Martinborough.

The norwester had stopped at the dark line of hills running north, but white summer clouds continued to roll across a big clean sky.

In Kansas I drew up outside Cliff and Bess's. There was no sign of life in the windows. I walked around the house and came back to lean against the car. For a short while I listened to the iron roof crack and stretch in the heat before I noticed something new on the lawn—a second letterbox marked with the letter "b." There was the old box and beside it this new clue that Cliff's life had finally parted company with Bess's. Into this letterbox I slipped the postcard of the Emperor.

One month later, in February, I received a letter from Kadris. Everything had fallen apart in Lushnje. Every time the doctor's son turned his head, another warehouse was looted.

He told a story about his neighbour who had joined in the looting of a truck outside of town. The neighbour had staggered off home with a heavy sack of grain, injuring his back in the process, only to discover he had looted a hundredweight sack of sugar.

Kadris came to the point. Shapallo had failed to make it through the winter. In the first week of January Savra ran out of fuel and wood, the ground froze, and Shapallo's emphysema grew steadily worse. Leila found him one morning bundled up in blankets propped against a wall. She had walked into Lushnje and left a message with Mister Gina. But it was another two days before Kadris got the message, and by then Shapallo was already buried in an unmarked grave behind the barracks of Savra's first exiles.

May 1992, Reuters in Tirana reports: Enver Hoxha's tomb has been opened and the body taken to another part of the city for reburial in a commoner's grave.

Acknowledgments and
Further Reading

The letter offering Lord Inchcape the Albanian throne (pages 97–98) is reproduced from *The Men Who Would Be King: A Look at Royalty in Exile*, by Nicholas Shakespeare (London: Sidgwick & Jackson, 1984).

Rose Wilder Lane's description of Tirana (page 26) is drawn from *Dorothy Thompson and Rose Wilder Lane: Forty Years of Friendship—Letters, 1921–1960*, edited by William Holtz (Columbia, Missouri: University of Missouri Press, 1991).

Other works consulted include:

Julian Amery. *Sons of the Eagle: A Study in Guerrilla War*. Toronto: Macmillan, 1948.

The Artful Albanian: The Memoirs of Enver Hoxha. Edited and introduced by Jon Halliday. London: Chatto & Windus, 1986; Topfield, Massachusetts: Salem House, 1987.

Bernd Jurgen Fischer. *King Zog and the Struggle for Stability in Albania*. Boulder, Colorado: East European Monographs (Columbia University Press, distributor), 1984.

Harry Hamm. *Albania: China's Beachhead in Europe*. London: Weidenfeld & Nicholson, 1963; New York: Praeger, 1963.

Gwen Robyns. *Geraldine of the Albanians: The Authorised Biography*. London: Muller, Blond & White, 1987.

Joseph Swire. *Albania: The Rise of a Kingdom*. London: Williams & Norgate, 1929; Salem, New Hampshire: Ayer, 1991.

————. *King Zog's Albania*. New York: Liveright, 1931.